Published by Time Inc. Books
225 Liberty Street
New York, NY 10281

FOOD & WINE is a trademark of Time Inc.
Affluent Media Group, registered in the
U.S. and other countries.

ISBN 13: 978-0-8487-5268-2

Library of Congress Control Number:
2017947383

Printed in the United States of America
10 9 8 7 6 5 4 3 2 1
First Edition 2017

EXECUTIVE EDITOR **Kate Heddings**
EDITOR **Susan Choung**
WRITER (CHAPTER INTROS) **Megan Krigbaum**
DESIGNER **Alisha Petro**
COPY EDITOR **Lisa Leventer**
PRODUCTION DIRECTOR **Joseph Colucci**
PRODUCTION MANAGERS **Stephanie
Thompson, John Markic**
EDITORIAL ASSISTANT **Dinavie Salazar**

FRONT COVER
Pork Milanese (recipe, p. 188)
PHOTOGRAPHER **Eva Kolenko**
FOOD STYLIST **Vivian Lui**
PROP STYLIST **Natasha Kolenko**

BACK COVER
Soufflé (recipe, p. 34)
PHOTOGRAPHER **Christina Holmes**
FOOD STYLIST **Simon Andrews**
STYLE EDITOR **Suzie Myers**
For additional photo contributors,
see page 268.

FOOD & WINE
EDITOR IN CHIEF **Nilou Motamed**
EXECUTIVE EDITOR **Dana Bowen**
EXECUTIVE WINE EDITOR **Ray Isle**
ART DIRECTOR **James Maikowski**
PHOTO EDITOR **Sara Parks**
PHOTO ASSISTANT **Rebecca Delman**

The Food & Wine Guide to Perfect Pairings

150+ Delicious Recipes
Matched with the World's
Most Popular Wines

FOOD&WINE
BOOKS

Contents

Lightly Sweet Wines

ROSÉ

REDS

Pinot Noir & Other Savory, Aromatic Reds

Sangiovese & Other Medium-Bodied, Tangy Reds

Syrah & Other Spicy, Full-Bodied Reds

Cabernet Sauvignon & Other Big Reds

Foreword

Here's a question: Is pairing wine with food a devilishly complex exercise, full of pitfalls for the unwary, or is it as simple as pouring wine you like alongside the food you like to eat?

The answer: It's a little bit of both. A great pairing can lift both the wine and accompanying dish into another plane, heightening flavors and aromas. When done right, it results in a kind of alchemy —a "1+1=3" intensity that will be both incredibly pleasurable and also truly memorable. At the same time, wine—any wine—will go better with your food than practically anything else you can drink. It's a beverage truly made to be on the table.

Should you worry or fret about what wine goes with what food? Of course not; life is too short! But should you experiment, have fun with the concept and find your favorite combos? Absolutely. And that's where this book comes in. We've chosen 10 of the most popular grape varieties and categories of wine, and selected their best food matches—the dishes that will truly make them sing. Have a bottle of terrific Sonoma Chardonnay on hand that you've been waiting to drink? Instead of stressing over what to serve with it, flip to page 97. You'll find 16 different recipes, from mushroom-and-Fontina-stuffed potatoes to a ham glazed with cider and cloves, each of which makes for a perfect pairing. Just returned from vacation in Napa Valley with a prize Cabernet? Invite some friends over and make them beef tenderloin with tomatoes, shallots and Maytag blue cheese (p. 254). We guarantee they'll be wowed.

There are over 150 remarkable recipes in these pages, from both F&W's Test Kitchen cooks as well as many of the world's star chefs. And we've added in-depth information about each wine variety, as well as similar choices that will work equally well for pairing. The result is an invaluable resource for anyone who loves both wine and food—not to mention a simple guide for giving the best dinner parties ever.

Ray Isle
Executive Wine Editor
FOOD & WINE

SPARKLING

CHAMPAGNE
& OTHER SPARKLING WINES

CHAMPAGNE The grande dame of all sparkling wines, Champagne comes from one place and one place only: the cool-climate region of Champagne, in northern France, respected worldwide for wines of outstanding complexity and ageability. That said, the traditional method employed to make sparkling wine in Champagne has been used around the world for centuries. This method hinges on a two-step fermentation process: The first is carried out in a tank or barrel (as with most still wines), and the second, by which the glorious bubbles are instilled into the wine, takes place in the bottle.

Champagnes are made using varying percentages of three grape varieties: Chardonnay, Pinot Noir and Pinot Meunier. Percentages depend on the desired style, from light and delicate all the way to rich and vinous. While actual French Champagne is not an inexpensive drink—the wines take a serious amount of time and manpower to make—nonvintage brut versions (dry wines that are blends of different years) can offer great value. Vintage-dated bottlings, along with Blanc de Blancs (white wines made from Chardonnay) and Blanc de Noirs (white wines made from red grapes), tend to be pricier; and the great têtes de cuvées such as Dom Pérignon and Cristal can be very pricey indeed.

There is no question that Champagne represents luxury and indulgence, but to in-the-know wine lovers, it's also fantastic with crispy fried chicken or a bowl of salty potato chips. (The bubbles interact with salt in an almost magical way.) While Champagne is certainly excellent with appetizers, it can be equally delicious throughout the entire meal. Sommeliers, in fact, love to say that Champagne goes well with everything. Whether that's absolutely true, there's no denying that it's tremendous with shellfish, scrambled eggs, creamy soups and pastas, fish and lighter meats.

PROSECCO Italy makes a handful of different sparkling wines (Franciacorta, Lambrusco, Moscato d'Asti), but its signature fizz is undeniably Prosecco, the lightly floral, fruit-forward sparkler from the regions just north of Venice. You will find it on tap in every *bacaro* in Venice's backstreets, served with antipasti like fresh salads and seafood, and now you'll see it on nearly every store shelf in the US, too. The best Proseccos are made with grapes from the steep slopes of the Conegliano Valdobbiadene, an area just south of the Alps that benefits from brilliant sun and cooling breezes. Prosecco can be made from a handful of different varieties, but the most important is a white grape called Glera. Prosecco winemakers utilize a much quicker (months versus years) process than Champagne producers for getting bubbles in their wine, called the Charmat method. In it, grapes are fermented as usual, then the juice is sealed in enormous pressurized stainless steel vats for the second fermentation. The result: frothy, approachable wines that are both affordable and light-hearted. A brunch go-to, Prosecco is otherwise best with lighter foods and starters.

CAVA While Cava can legally come from anywhere in Spain, the greatest examples are made in a part of Catalonia called Penedès, south and west of Barcelona. The area has been producing sparkling wine, using the same method as Champagne, since Josep Raventós bottled the first Cava in the late 1800s. Here, producers make dry sparkling wines with varying amounts of three native Spanish grape varieties: Macabeo, Xarel-lo and Parellada. Most Cava is nonvintage, but a few top wineries are beginning to invest in making *reservas* (aged for at least 15 months on the lees), an exciting development in the Cava world. At the same time, rosé Cava, created by blending in a percentage of red grape juice, is on the rise, giving breadth to a wine landscape that for a long time was quite homogeneous. Classic Cava has a distinct green apple perkiness and earthy depth that's matched by soft bubbles. It goes as well with cheese and charcuterie, such as Spain's classic jamón Iberico, as it does with seafood, salads and crispy fried snacks.

Grilled Escarole Toasts with Trout Roe

Winemaker Maggie Harrison of Antica Terra in Dundee, Oregon, transforms simple escarole into dinner party–worthy toasts: She tops each one with crème fraîche and trout roe, which is smaller, milder and less salty than salmon roe.

TIME **45 min total**	MAKES **6 servings**	CONTRIBUTED BY **Maggie Harrison**

Two 10- to 12-oz. heads of escarole

½ cup extra-virgin olive oil, plus more for brushing

1 Tbsp. chopped thyme

2 garlic cloves, minced

Kosher salt and pepper

Eighteen ½-inch-thick baguette slices, cut on a wide diagonal

Crème fraîche and trout roe, for serving

STEP 1 Light a grill. Fill a large bowl with cold water. Holding the escarole by the root end, dip the heads in the water to release any dirt between the leaves. Shake off the excess water.

STEP 2 In a small bowl, whisk the ½ cup of olive oil with the thyme and garlic. Brush the escarole with garlic oil and season with salt and pepper. Grill over moderate heat until charred outside and tender within, about 20 minutes; brush a few times with garlic oil during grilling. Transfer to a work surface and let cool, then coarsely chop.

STEP 3 Brush the baguette slices with olive oil and season with salt and pepper. Grill until lightly charred on both sides, about 2 minutes.

STEP 4 In a large bowl, toss the escarole with any remaining garlic oil; season with salt and pepper. Top the toasts with the escarole, crème fraîche and roe and serve.

WINE TIP

Crisp Champagne is an outstanding match for the briny trout roe, rich crème fraîche and garlicky grilled bitter greens here.

Tuna Briks

Briks are small, triangular, savory pastries made throughout Tunisia with fillings that range from meat and egg to mashed potato. A universal ingredient, though, is harissa, a fiery North African chile paste. This delicious version is wrapped in store-bought phyllo dough and filled with scallions, capers and canned tuna.

TIME	MAKES	CONTRIBUTED BY
30 min total	**8 small pies**	**Kay Chun**

Two 7-oz. cans tuna packed in water, drained well and flaked

¼ cup finely chopped scallions

¼ cup chopped drained capers

¼ cup chopped parsley

¼ cup extra-virgin olive oil

2 Tbsp. harissa

Kosher salt and pepper

6 sheets of phyllo dough

1 large egg, beaten

Canola oil, for frying

STEP 1 In a medium bowl, combine the tuna, scallions, capers, parsley, olive oil and harissa. Season with salt and pepper and mix gently.

STEP 2 On a work surface, make 2 stacks of 3 phyllo sheets each. Cut each stack crosswise into four 4-by-12-inch strips. Work with 1 strip at a time, keeping the rest covered with a damp kitchen towel. Place a heaping ¼ cup of the tuna filling at the end of a strip closest to you. Brush the edge of the other end with the beaten egg. Fold the corner of the phyllo over the filling to form a triangle. Continue folding the triangle up and over itself until you reach the end of the strip; press to adhere. Repeat with the remaining phyllo strips, filling and beaten egg.

STEP 3 In a large cast-iron skillet, heat ¼ inch of canola oil until shimmering. Fry 4 of the phyllo triangles over moderately low heat, turning occasionally, until golden and crisp, 3 to 4 minutes. Transfer the briks to a paper towel–lined plate to drain. Repeat with the 4 remaining phyllo triangles. Serve hot.

Prep Ahead

The filled phyllo triangles can be refrigerated for up to 3 hours before frying.

Everything Twists

These fun puff pastry twists get the "everything" bagel treatment. Bonus: They can be frozen unbaked between sheets of parchment for up to one month .

TIME	MAKES	CONTRIBUTED BY
20 min active; 1 hr 20 min total	**About 32 twists**	**Melissa Rubel Jacobson**

1½ Tbsp. sesame seeds

1 Tbsp. poppy seeds

2 tsp. caraway seeds

1½ Tbsp. dehydrated chopped onion

1½ tsp. coarse sea salt

1 tsp. garlic powder

One 14-oz. package all-butter puff pastry, thawed if frozen but still cold

1 egg beaten with 1½ tsp. water

STEP 1 In a small bowl, mix the sesame, poppy and caraway seeds with the onion, salt and garlic powder.

STEP 2 Line 3 large baking sheets with parchment paper. On a floured work surface, roll out the puff pastry to an 11-by-14-inch rectangle; cut in half lengthwise. Brush with the egg wash and sprinkle evenly with the seed mixture. Cut the pastry crosswise

into ¾-inch-wide strips. Twist the strips and transfer to the baking sheets, leaving 2 inches in between. Freeze until firm, 30 minutes.

STEP 3 Preheat the oven to 375°. Bake the twists for about 22 minutes, until golden; shift the sheets from top to bottom and front to back halfway through baking. Let stand until cool enough to handle, about 10 minutes. Transfer to a platter and serve.

Mexican Corn Popcorn

"My absolute favorite thing to pair with Champagne is popcorn," says Jen Pelka of The Riddler Champagne bar in San Francisco, where this spicy version is a signature snack.

TIME	MAKES	CONTRIBUTED BY
30 min total	**6 servings**	**Jen Pelka**

½ cup white cheese powder, such as King Arthur Vermont Cheese Powder (see Note)

2 Tbsp. kosher salt

1 tsp. chipotle chile powder

1 tsp. crushed dried cilantro

½ tsp. ground dried lime zest or 1 tsp. finely grated lime zest

¼ tsp. cayenne

⅓ cup canola oil

¾ cup popping corn

4 Tbsp. unsalted butter, melted

STEP 1 In a small bowl, mix the cheese powder with the salt, chile powder, cilantro, lime zest and cayenne.

STEP 2 In a large saucepan, combine the canola oil and popping corn. Cover and cook over moderately high heat until the corn starts to pop. Shake the pan and cook, shaking occasionally, until the corn stops popping, 3 to 5 minutes. Transfer

to a large bowl, add the melted butter and toss to coat. Add the cheese mixture, toss again and serve.

Note
King Arthur Vermont Cheese Powder is available at kingarthurflour.com.

Potato–Apple Pancakes

Tart Granny Smith apple and fresh dill punch up the flavor of these crispy potato pancakes. They're fabulous on their own or with sour cream or slices of smoked salmon.

TIME **25 min total**	MAKES **12 pancakes**	CONTRIBUTED BY **Kay Chun** 📷

2 baking potatoes, peeled and grated on the large holes of a box grater

1 Granny Smith apple, peeled and grated on the large holes of a box grater

¼ cup chopped dill

3 Tbsp. all-purpose flour

Kosher salt and pepper

6 Tbsp. canola oil

Sour cream, for serving

STEP 1 Squeeze all the excess water from the potatoes and apple and place them in a medium bowl. Add the dill and flour, season with salt and pepper and toss to coat thoroughly.

STEP 2 In a large nonstick skillet, heat 1 tablespoon of the oil. Scoop four ¼-cup mounds of the potato mixture into the skillet; press gently to flatten. Cook over moderately high heat, turning once and adding 1 tablespoon of oil, until golden and crisp, about 2 minutes per side. Drain briefly on a paper towel–lined plate. Repeat with the remaining potato mixture and oil. Serve with sour cream.

Roasted Fingerling Potato & Pressed Caviar Canapés

For this easy yet impressive hors d'oeuvre, master chef Jacques Pépin tops roasted fingerling potatoes with sour cream and a diamond-shaped garnish of pressed caviar.

TIME **20 min active; 35 min total**	MAKES **4 servings**	CONTRIBUTED BY **Jacques Pépin**

10 fingerling potatoes, scrubbed and halved lengthwise

1 Tbsp. extra-virgin olive oil

Kosher salt and pepper

2 Tbsp. pressed caviar (2 oz.; californiacaviar.com)

½ cup sour cream

Chives cut into twenty 1-inch lengths, for garnish

STEP 1 Preheat the oven to 400°. On a large rimmed baking sheet, toss the potatoes with the oil; season with salt and pepper. Arrange the potatoes cut side down and roast for about 25 minutes, until tender and browned on the bottoms. Let cool to warm.

STEP 2 Meanwhile, roll out the caviar between 2 sheets of plastic wrap to a 5-by-6-inch rectangle about ⅛ inch thick. Cut the sheet into 20 diamonds or rectangles.

STEP 3 Transfer the potatoes to a platter cut side up and dollop sour cream on each. Top with the caviar diamonds and garnish with the chives. Serve right away.

Shrimp Cakes

These tender little shrimp cakes, spiked with scallions, lemon zest and smoked paprika, are addictive, especially with the spicy mayo that's served on the side.

TIME	MAKES	CONTRIBUTED BY
30 min total	**4 servings**	**Justin Chapple**

½ cup mayonnaise

1 Tbsp. hot sauce

1 lb. shelled and deveined shrimp, chopped

¾ cup panko

2 large eggs

3 Tbsp. finely chopped scallions

1 tsp. finely grated lemon zest

¾ tsp. smoked paprika

Kosher salt and pepper

¼ cup extra-virgin olive oil

Lemon wedges, for serving

STEP 1 In a small bowl, whisk the mayonnaise with the hot sauce.

STEP 2 In a large bowl, mix the chopped shrimp with the panko, eggs, scallions, lemon zest, smoked paprika, 1 teaspoon of salt

and ½ teaspoon of pepper. Form the mixture into eight ¾-inch-thick cakes.

STEP 3 In a large skillet, heat the olive oil. In batches, add the shrimp cakes and cook over moderately high heat, turning once, until browned and cooked through, about 4 minutes. Transfer to plates and serve with the spicy mayonnaise and lemon.

Hand–Cut Fries with Smoked Aioli

Serving homemade fries will earn you favorite-cook status. Double-frying them ensures that the potatoes are ultra-crispy on the outside and fluffy on the inside.

WINE TIP Salt and fat both love Champagne (and vice versa)–the wine's high acidity and the prickle of those bubbles are the ideal preparation for the next bite, and the next, and the next, and so on.

TIME	MAKES	CONTRIBUTED BY
1 hr total	**6 servings**	**Michael Paley**

¾ cup mayonnaise

1 garlic clove

1 tsp. pimentón de la Vera (smoked Spanish paprika)

1 tsp. fresh lemon juice

1 Tbsp. plus 2 tsp. finely chopped flat-leaf parsley

Kosher salt and pepper

Vegetable oil, for frying

3 large, very firm baking potatoes (about 2 lbs.), peeled and cut into ½-inch-thick sticks

STEP 1 In a food processor, puree the mayonnaise with the garlic, smoked paprika and lemon juice. Stir in 2 teaspoons of the parsley and season with salt and pepper. Scrape the aioli into a small bowl and refrigerate until ready to use.

STEP 2 In a large saucepan, heat 1 inch of oil to 250°. In a large bowl, rinse the potatoes and pat thoroughly dry. Working in batches, fry the potatoes until they

are almost tender and look dry on the outside, about 6 minutes. Transfer to paper towels to drain.

STEP 3 Increase the oil temperature to 350°. Cook the fries in batches until golden and crisp, about 3 minutes. Transfer to paper towels to drain and immediately season with salt. Sprinkle the fries with the remaining 1 tablespoon of parsley and serve with the smoked aioli.

Provoleta with Oregano & Tomatoes

Argentinean grill genius Francis Mallmann sears provolone cheese in a cast-iron skillet over a live fire until it's crisp, browned and melty, but you can bake it in the oven as well.

TIME **15 min total**	MAKES **4 servings**	CONTRIBUTED BY **Francis Mallmann**

One 1-inch-thick slice of provolone cheese (½ lb.)

2 Tbsp. small oregano leaves

½ tsp. crushed red pepper

6 grape tomatoes, halved

Sea salt

Basil leaves, for garnish

Crusty bread, for serving

Preheat the oven to 450°. Heat a cast-iron skillet until hot. Add the cheese and sprinkle with 1 tablespoon of the oregano and ¼ teaspoon of the crushed red pepper. Cook over moderate heat until the cheese begins to melt and brown on the bottom, about 2 minutes. Flip the cheese and cook until the bottom begins to melt and brown, about 2 minutes. Sprinkle all over with the remaining oregano and crushed red pepper and top with the grape tomatoes. Transfer to the oven and bake until the cheese is melted and the tomatoes are warmed through, about 4 minutes. Season with sea salt, garnish with basil and serve with bread.

Spaghetti with Brussels Sprouts & Sausage

Thinly sliced brussels sprouts add an earthy note to this superfast pasta with sausage. Panko mixed in with the spaghetti gives the dish a fabulous crunch.

TIME **20 min total**	MAKES **2 servings**	CONTRIBUTED BY **Kay Chun**

½ lb. spaghetti

¼ cup extra-virgin olive oil, plus more for drizzling

½ lb. brussels sprouts, thinly sliced (about 3 cups)

½ lb. loose pork sausage

1 cup panko

2 Tbsp. snipped chives

Kosher salt and pepper

Lemon wedges, for serving

In a pot of salted boiling water, cook the pasta until al dente. Meanwhile, in a large nonstick skillet, heat the ¼ cup of olive oil. Add the brussels sprouts and sausage and cook over moderately high heat, stirring, until the sausage is browned and cooked through, about 5 minutes. Stir in the panko and cook until crisp, 3 minutes. Stir in the chives and season with salt and pepper. Drain the spaghetti. Top with the brussels sprout mixture, drizzle with olive oil and serve with lemon wedges.

Celery Root Bisque with Walnut-Parsley Gremolata

Resourceful cooks in Italy know to save Parmesan rinds to toss into soups, deepening their richness. Similarly, sneaking a small piece of Parmigiano-Reggiano into the broth gives this creamy bisque an umami boost. Instead of croutons, a vibrant walnut-and-parsley gremolata garnish adds another layer of flavor and texture.

TIME **45 min active; 1 hr 30 min total**	MAKES **8 servings**	CONTRIBUTED BY **Kay Chun**

1 Tbsp. unsalted butter

1 large leek, white and light green parts only, thinly sliced

5 garlic cloves, crushed

2½ lbs. celery root, peeled and cut into 1-inch dice (8 cups)

One 2-inch chunk of Parmigiano-Reggiano cheese (1 oz.), plus ¼ cup freshly grated cheese

2 cups chicken stock or low-sodium broth

½ cup walnuts

¼ cup extra-virgin olive oil

½ cup coarsely chopped parsley

½ cup heavy cream

Kosher salt and pepper

STEP 1 In a large saucepan, melt the butter. Add the leek and garlic and cook over moderate heat, stirring occasionally, until softened, about 5 minutes. Add the celery root, Parmesan chunk, stock and 5 cups of water and bring to a simmer. Cover and cook over moderately low heat, stirring occasionally, until the celery root is tender, about 40 minutes.

STEP 2 Meanwhile, preheat the oven to 375°. Spread the walnuts in a pie plate and toast for 5 to 7 minutes, until golden. Let cool, then finely chop and transfer to a bowl. Add the oil, parsley and grated cheese and mix well.

STEP 3 In a blender, puree the soup in 2 batches until very smooth. Pour into a clean saucepan and stir in the heavy cream; season with salt and pepper and reheat if necessary. Serve topped with the walnut gremolata.

Make Ahead
The soup can be refrigerated for up to 2 days.

WINE
TIP

Cavas from Spain tend to have an earthy note, making them ideal with nutty cheeses or nuts, like the walnuts in this gremolata topping.

Broccoli–Spinach Soup with Crispy Broccoli Florets & Croutons

Given this soup's supremely silky texture, you'll think it's made with cream, but that lushness actually comes from a cooked potato pureed into the broth. For contrast, the soup is topped with crispy broccoli florets and croutons.

TIME	MAKES	CONTRIBUTED BY
45 min active; 1 hr 15 min total	**8 to 10 servings**	**Justin Chapple** 📷 PAGE 31

¼ cup plus 2 Tbsp. extra-virgin olive oil

1 medium yellow onion, finely chopped

2 large garlic cloves, sliced

Kosher salt and pepper

2 cups chicken stock or low-sodium broth

One 8-oz. baking potato, peeled and cut into 1-inch pieces

2 lbs. broccoli, stems peeled and sliced, florets cut into ½-inch pieces

One 5-oz. package baby spinach

4 oz. sourdough or ciabatta bread, cut into ½-inch dice

1 Tbsp. red wine vinegar

Snipped chives, for garnish

STEP 1 Preheat the oven to 400°. In a large pot, heat ¼ cup of the olive oil. Add the onion and garlic and season with salt and pepper. Cook over moderate heat, stirring occasionally, until softened and just starting to brown, 6 to 8 minutes. Add 2 cups of water and the stock, potato, broccoli stems and two-thirds of the florets. Bring to a boil over high heat, then simmer over moderate heat, stirring occasionally, until the potato and broccoli are very soft, about 30 minutes. Stir in the spinach until wilted.

STEP 2 Meanwhile, on one side of a large rimmed baking sheet, toss the remaining broccoli florets with 1 tablespoon of the olive oil and season with salt and pepper. In a medium bowl, toss the bread with the remaining 1 tablespoon of oil and season with salt and pepper. Bake the broccoli florets for 10 minutes. Spread the bread on the other half of the baking sheet and bake for about 10 minutes, until the florets and croutons are browned and crisp.

STEP 3 Working in batches, puree the soup in a blender until very smooth, 1 to 2 minutes. Stir in the vinegar and season with salt and pepper. Ladle the soup into bowls and top with the crispy broccoli and croutons. Garnish with snipped chives and serve.

Make Ahead
The soup can be refrigerated overnight. The broccoli florets and croutons can be made early in the day and stored at room temperature.

Asparagus & Bok Choy Frittata

When making a frittata, pretty much anything goes—even ingredients that aren't traditionally Italian, like bok choy. You can cook the eggs on the stove or in the oven, but be sure to use moderate heat so they don't cook too quickly and become rubbery—a faux pas in any culture.

TIME **20 min active; 45 min total**	MAKES **4 servings**	CONTRIBUTED BY **F&W Test Kitchen**

2 Tbsp. vegetable oil

3 scallions, thinly sliced

1 tsp. finely grated peeled fresh ginger

1 garlic clove, minced

1 small head of bok choy (about ¾ lb.), cut into 1-inch pieces

¾ lb. asparagus, trimmed and cut into 1-inch pieces

¾ tsp. kosher salt

9 large eggs, beaten

¼ tsp. black pepper

1 tsp. Asian sesame oil

STEP 1 Preheat the oven to 325°. In a medium cast-iron or ovenproof nonstick skillet, heat the vegetable oil. Add the scallions, ginger and garlic and cook over moderate heat, stirring, until fragrant, about 30 seconds. Add the bok choy and cook, stirring, until the leaves wilt, about 2 minutes. Add the asparagus and ½ teaspoon of the salt and continue to cook, stirring occasionally, until the vegetables are almost tender, about 3 minutes more.

STEP 2 Evenly distribute the vegetables in the skillet, then add the eggs, pepper and the remaining ¼ teaspoon of salt. Cook the frittata over moderate heat, without stirring, until the edge starts to set, about 2 minutes. Transfer to the oven and bake until the frittata is firm, about 25 minutes. Drizzle the sesame oil on top and serve.

WINE TIP

Champagne and eggs are a classic combo—the bubbles and acidity cut through that eggy richness. For a less expensive pairing, seek out sparkling wines from other parts of France, such as Crémant du Jura and Crémant de Bourgogne.

Cauliflower & Gruyère Soufflé

Claudine Pépin, daughter of renowned chef Jacques Pépin, says her go-to dinner-party dish was inspired by her father's famous soufflé. "Years ago, I changed the recipe— I took out some of the cheese and replaced it with pureed cauliflower," she says. "Now, heaven forbid, in a completely un-French way, I serve this soufflé as a side dish—but never to my father."

WINE
TIP

Cruciferous vegetables like cauliflower and broccoli can be tough to pair with wine, but sparkling wines help mellow their sulfury notes.

TIME **30 min active; 1 hr 45 min total**	MAKES **6 to 8 servings**	CONTRIBUTED BY **Claudine Pépin**

½ lb. cauliflower florets, cut into 1-inch pieces

1 stick unsalted butter

⅓ cup all-purpose flour

2 cups whole milk

Kosher salt and pepper

6 oz. Gruyère cheese, shredded (2 lightly packed cups)

2 Tbsp. finely chopped chives

6 large eggs

STEP 1 In a medium saucepan of salted boiling water, cook the cauliflower until very tender, about 7 minutes. Drain well and pat dry. In a medium bowl, puree the cauliflower with a potato masher or fork. Transfer the cauliflower to a colander and let drain until cooled completely.

STEP 2 Meanwhile, preheat the oven to 350°. Grease a 6-cup soufflé dish with 1 tablespoon of the butter and set it on a rimmed baking sheet. In a medium saucepan, melt the remaining 7 tablespoons of butter. Add the flour and whisk over moderate heat until bubbling, about 3 minutes. Gradually whisk in the milk and bring to a boil. Simmer over moderately low heat, whisking, until thickened and no floury taste remains, about 7 minutes. Season the béchamel with salt and pepper. Scrape into a large bowl and let cool, stirring occasionally.

STEP 3 Stir the cauliflower puree into the béchamel, then fold in the cheese and chives. In a medium bowl, beat the eggs until frothy, then gently fold them into the cauliflower béchamel. Scrape the soufflé base into the prepared dish and bake for about 1 hour and 10 minutes, until puffed and browned; serve right away.

Oysters on the Half Shell with Spiced Cucumbers

Dylan Fultineer, the chef at Rappahannock in Richmond, Virginia, is always dreaming up new ways to show off Chesapeake Bay oysters. Topping the raw oysters with a spicy, tangy cucumber relish is one of his favorite ways to highlight their flavor.

TIME **30 min total**	MAKES **1 dozen oysters**	CONTRIBUTED BY **Dylan Fultineer**

1 tsp. coriander seeds

¼ cup finely diced peeled Asian pear

¼ cup peeled, seeded and finely diced cucumber

1 serrano chile, seeded and minced

1 Tbsp. minced cilantro

1 Tbsp. fresh lime juice

1 tsp. minced candied ginger

1 tsp. Asian fish sauce

1 tsp. extra-virgin olive oil

Kosher salt and pepper

12 freshly shucked oysters on the half shell, such as Rappahannocks

Crushed ice, for serving

STEP 1 In a small skillet, toast the coriander seeds over moderate heat until fragrant, 2 minutes. Let cool, then coarsely crush the seeds in a mortar. In a small bowl, mix the crushed coriander with all of the remaining ingredients except the oysters and ice.

STEP 2 Arrange the oysters on crushed ice. Spoon some of the topping on each one and serve right away, passing additional topping at the table.

WINE **TIP**

Oysters are best with extremely dry, almost steely wines– look for Champagnes labeled "extra-brut" or "zero dosage."

Spinach & Prosciutto Ravioli

As a stuffing for her supple ravioli, Missy Robbins, chef at Lilia in Brooklyn, mixes spinach and prosciutto with fresh ricotta and mascarpone. Her recipe can be made ahead: Simply freeze the uncooked ravioli on a baking sheet in a single layer, then transfer them to a large resealable plastic bag when they're solid. They'll keep for up to one month.

TIME	MAKES	CONTRIBUTED BY
1 hr 30 min active; 3 hr total	**6 to 8 servings**	**Missy Robbins**

FILLING

½ lb. prosciutto, sliced ½ inch thick

1 lb. curly spinach, stems discarded

6 oz. fresh ricotta cheese

6 oz. fresh mascarpone cheese

2 large egg yolks

1 cup freshly grated Parmigiano-Reggiano cheese

Kosher salt

PASTA

2½ cups 00 flour

1 tsp. kosher salt

12 large egg yolks

Semolina flour, for dusting

1 stick plus 2 Tbsp. unsalted butter, cut into thin slices

4 oz. curly spinach, coarsely chopped (4 cups)

2 tsp. fennel pollen or ½ tsp. ground fennel

½ cup freshly grated Parmigiano-Reggiano cheese

STEP 1 MAKE THE FILLING Dice the prosciutto and transfer to a bowl. Freeze until very firm, about 30 minutes. In a food processor, pulse the chilled prosciutto until finely chopped, about 30 seconds. Return to the bowl.

STEP 2 Meanwhile, in a pot of salted boiling water, blanch the spinach until just tender, about 1 minute. Transfer to a colander and let cool slightly. Press out all of the excess water and coarsely chop the spinach; you should have about ½ cup.

STEP 3 In a medium bowl, whisk the ricotta until smooth. Add the prosciutto along with the chopped spinach, the mascarpone, egg yolks and Parmesan; stir well. Season with salt. Cover the filling with plastic wrap and refrigerate until firm, about 30 minutes.

STEP 4 MAKE THE PASTA In a large bowl, whisk the 00 flour with the salt; make a well in the center. Add the egg yolks and 1 tablespoon of water to the well and mix. Using a fork, gradually incorporate the flour into the wet ingredients until a shaggy dough forms. Scrape the dough out onto a work surface very lightly dusted with semolina flour and knead until stiff but smooth, about 5 minutes. Wrap in plastic and let rest at room temperature until softened, about 45 minutes.

STEP 5 Generously dust a work surface with semolina flour. Line a rimmed baking sheet with parchment paper and dust with semolina flour. Divide the pasta dough into 4 pieces and work with 1 at a time; keep the rest covered. Press the dough to flatten. Using a hand-cranked pasta machine and starting at the widest setting, run the dough twice through each of the first 5 settings, then run it once through the sixth setting. Cut the sheet in half; run each half through the thinnest setting one time. Transfer the sheets to the prepared work surface.

STEP 6 Lay 1 pasta sheet on a work surface with a long edge facing you. Spoon eight 1-teaspoon-size balls of filling in each of 2 rows on the sheet, allowing 1 inch of space between them. Very lightly brush the dough around the filling with water. Place the second pasta sheet on top. Using your fingers, press the dough around each mound of filling. Using a 2-inch fluted cutter, stamp out the ravioli; transfer to the semolina-dusted baking sheet. Cover with a clean tea towel. Repeat with the remaining dough and filling to make 64 ravioli.

STEP 7 In a pot of salted boiling water, cook the ravioli in 2 batches until the edges are tender, about 2 minutes. Using a slotted spoon, transfer to a shallow bowl. Reserve 1 cup of the cooking water.

STEP 8 Melt 4 tablespoons of the butter in each of 2 large skillets. Add ½ cup of the pasta water and half of the chopped spinach to each skillet and cook over moderately high heat until the spinach is just wilted, about 1 minute. Add half of the ravioli to each skillet and cook, stirring gently, until they are coated in butter. Using a slotted spoon, transfer the ravioli and spinach to a large serving bowl. Scrape the remaining liquid from 1 large skillet into the other. Add the remaining 2 tablespoons of butter to the skillet along with 1 teaspoon of the fennel pollen and ¼ cup of the cheese. Cook over moderate heat, swirling the pan gently, until the butter has melted and the sauce has thickened slightly, about 1 minute. Scrape the sauce over the ravioli. Sprinkle with the remaining fennel pollen and cheese and serve immediately.

Extra-Crispy Fried Chicken

To make his phenomenal fried chicken, Food Network star Tyler Florence first bakes it low and slow, so it's juicy. Then he coats the chicken pieces in seasoned flour and fries them in oil that's been flavored with garlic and herbs.

TIME **1 hr 15 min active; 4 hr 30 min total**	MAKES **6 to 8 servings**	CONTRIBUTED BY **Tyler Florence**

¼ cup plus 2 Tbsp. kosher salt

¼ cup freshly ground pepper

¼ cup extra-virgin olive oil

1½ Tbsp. minced rosemary, plus 4 medium sprigs

1½ Tbsp. minced thyme, plus 4 sprigs

1½ Tbsp. minced sage, plus 4 sprigs

5 minced bay leaves, preferably fresh, plus 5 whole leaves

3 garlic cloves, minced, plus 1 head broken into cloves

Two 3-lb. whole chickens

1 qt. buttermilk

1 Tbsp. hot sauce, such as Tabasco

1 tsp. sugar

Grapeseed or vegetable oil, for frying

2 cups all-purpose flour

½ cup rice flour

¼ cup garlic powder

¼ cup onion powder

Flaky sea salt, for sprinkling

Lemon wedges, for serving

STEP 1 Preheat the oven to 200°. In a small bowl, whisk 3 tablespoons of the kosher salt with 2 tablespoons of the pepper, the olive oil and the minced rosemary, thyme, sage, bay leaves and garlic. Rub the mixture all over the chickens and set them in a roasting pan. Roast for about 2½ hours, until an instant-read thermometer inserted in the inner thighs registers 150°. Let the chickens cool, then cut each into 10 pieces. (You should have 4 drumsticks, 4 thighs, 4 wings and 8 breast quarters.)

STEP 2 In a very large bowl, whisk the buttermilk with the hot sauce and sugar. Add the chicken pieces and toss well. Cover and refrigerate for 1 hour.

STEP 3 In a large saucepan, heat 2 inches of grapeseed oil to 375° with the rosemary, thyme and sage sprigs, the 5 whole bay leaves and the head of garlic. When the herbs are crispy and the garlic is golden, transfer to a paper towel–lined plate.

STEP 4 Meanwhile, in a large bowl, whisk the all-purpose and rice flours with the garlic and onion powders. Whisk in the remaining 3 tablespoons of kosher salt and 2 tablespoons of pepper.

STEP 5 Remove half of the chicken pieces from the buttermilk, letting the excess drip back into the bowl. Dredge the chicken in the seasoned flour, patting it on lightly so it adheres. Fry the chicken over high heat, turning occasionally, until golden and an instant-read thermometer inserted in the thickest part of each piece registers 160°, about 6 minutes for the breasts and 8 minutes for the wings, thighs and drumsticks. Transfer the fried chicken to a paper towel–lined baking sheet to drain. Let the oil return to 375° before you coat and fry the remaining chicken. Transfer the chicken to a platter and garnish with the fried garlic and herbs. Sprinkle with flaky sea salt and serve right away, with lemon wedges.

Veal Meatballs with Mustard Greens

For this easy skillet meal, Georgia chef Hugh Acheson amps up tender veal meatballs with fennel seeds, mustard and chipotle powder. After browning the meatballs, he simmers them with stock to keep them moist.

TIME **45 min total**	MAKES **4 servings**	CONTRIBUTED BY **Hugh Acheson**

¼ cup extra-virgin olive oil

1 cup minced onion

2 garlic cloves, minced

½ tsp. ground fennel seeds

¼ tsp. mustard powder

¼ tsp. crushed red pepper

¼ tsp. ground coriander

¼ tsp. chipotle or other smoked chile powder

1 lb. ground veal

½ cup fresh breadcrumbs (2 oz.)

¼ cup heavy cream

1 large egg, lightly beaten

½ tsp. kosher salt

½ lb. mustard greens, thick stems discarded and leaves chopped

⅓ cup chicken stock or low-sodium broth

STEP 1 In a medium skillet, heat 2 tablespoons of the olive oil until shimmering. Add the onion and cook over moderately high heat, stirring occasionally, until softened and starting to brown, 5 minutes. Stir in the garlic, fennel seeds, mustard powder, crushed red pepper, coriander and chile powder and cook, stirring, until fragrant, about 2 minutes; let cool.

STEP 2 In a large bowl, mix the cooled onion mixture with the veal, breadcrumbs, cream, egg and salt. Form into 1½-inch meatballs and transfer to a rimmed baking sheet.

STEP 3 In a large skillet, heat the remaining 2 tablespoons of olive oil until shimmering. Add the meatballs and cook over moderately high heat, turning, until browned all over, 5 minutes. Gently push the meatballs to one side of the skillet. Spoon off all but 2 tablespoons of the fat from the pan, then add the mustard greens and stock. Cover and cook over moderate heat until the greens are wilted, 4 minutes. Spoon the meatballs and greens into bowls and serve.

Prep Ahead
The meatballs can be prepared through Step 2 and refrigerated overnight. Bring to room temperature before proceeding.

WHITES

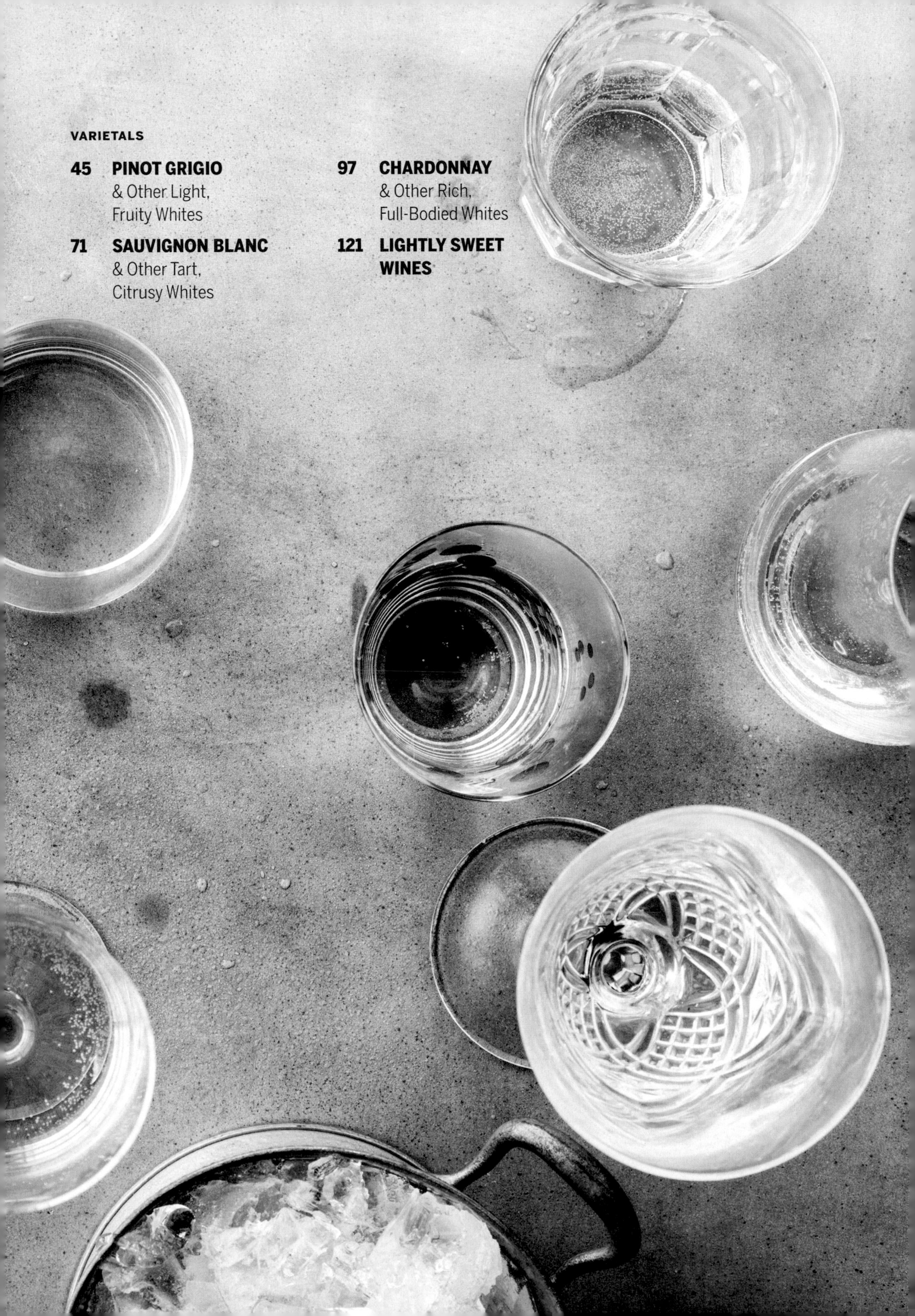

VARIETALS

PINOT GRIGIO
& OTHER LIGHT, FRUITY WHITES

PINOT GRIGIO Made in a thoughtful way from grapes grown in the right place, Pinot Grigio can be a lovely, fruit-forward, light-bodied white wine. But for much of the past two decades, its reputation has suffered, thanks to an ocean of anemic, flavorless versions produced by industrial wineries around the world. Even so, there are two areas that have traditionally excelled with this grape, and continue to produce wines that deserve respect and attention: northeastern Italy's Alto Adige and Friuli, and eastern France's Alsace (where the grape goes by the name Pinot Gris). Additionally, there are several New World wine regions, among them Oregon and New Zealand, that are well worth keeping an eye on when it comes to Pinot Gris.

The differences in Pinot Grigio from one place to the next are remarkable. In Italy, Pinot Grigio is fresh, citrusy and crisp, with vibrant, food-loving acidity derived from high altitudes and Alpine air. Pair these wines with green salads with zesty vinaigrettes, raw seafood and flaky white fish. Over in Alsace, with its long, sunny growing season, Pinot Gris takes on an entirely different flavor profile. The brightness is still there, but the wines are weightier, with ripe pear fruit and spice notes. Often Alsace versions will have a touch of sweetness (as do New Zealand's; Oregon's tend to be dry), which is

a nice foil to the wine's focused acidity. Alsace Pinot Gris is fantastic with cheese, meatier fish and poultry; locals even serve it with lighter pork dishes because it has enough heft to stand up to something with a little fat.

DRY RIESLING A lot of people claim not to like Riesling, typically citing its sweetness as the problem. But they're missing out—the truth is that there are a great many Rieslings that aren't sweet at all, bone-dry wines that are exceptional with food. In fact, one of Riesling's constant dilemmas is that when it comes from certain (very important) places, particularly Germany, the label won't necessarily tell you whether it's sweet or not (this is where a wine store clerk or sommelier comes in handy).

The good news is there's more and more delicious dry Riesling on the market from around the globe, offering mouthwatering acidity and concentrated fruit flavors. The Eden and Clare Valleys of Australia, for instance, have been producing stellar dry Riesling for decades. Other places to seek out dry Riesling are New York's Finger Lakes, Washington state (sometimes), Austria and Alsace. This style of Riesling is incredibly versatile when it comes to pairing; try it with everything from citrusy salads to roast chicken or pork to grilled fish.

VINHO VERDE Vinho Verde has come to be known as Portugal's cheap and spritzy signature white. There's no shame in that: A cold Vinho Verde on a hot day is one of the most refreshing wine experiences to be had. But as more and more bottles come to the US, it's also obvious that light-bodied, citrusy, unoaked Vinho Verde can offer more than that. Produced in the northwest corner of the country, in the Minho region (bordered by the Douro and Minho Rivers), Vinho Verde can be made from numerous white grape varieties, mostly Alvarinho, Arinto and Loureiro; a few rare outliers are even made from red grapes, like Vinhão and Azal Tinto. Most bottlings are blends, but a few ambitious producers are exploring single-variety expressions, calling on the diversity of the region's many vineyards.

While a good number of Vinhos Verdes retain a little bit of effervescence and a signature lemony-limy vibe—nothing wrong with that; they may be the most perfect beach wines ever—others are made in a more complex, ambitious style, recalling in some ways top Muscadets from France or Grüner Veltliners from Austria. Universally, though, the region's close proximity to the Atlantic Ocean gives the wines a salty lift that's outstanding with shellfish, fresh vegetables and lighter poultry dishes.

Radicchio Salad with Manchego Vinaigrette

This salad is a favorite of the Food52 online community because it tastes like it takes much more work than it really does. Flavoring the vinegar by soaking an onion in it results in a deeply delicious vinaigrette, with none of the harshness that can often come from raw onion. Food52 creative director Kristen Miglore adapted the recipe from the *Toro Bravo* cookbook by John Gorham and Liz Crain.

TIME **20 min active; 1 hr 20 min total**	MAKES **8 to 10 servings**	CONTRIBUTED BY **Kristen Miglore**

¼ cup balsamic vinegar

¼ cup sherry vinegar

1 red onion, chopped

3 heads of radicchio (2 lbs.)— halved, cored and chopped into 1-inch pieces

1 Tbsp. honey

¾ cup extra-virgin olive oil

6 oz. Manchego cheese, shredded (1½ cups)

Kosher salt and pepper

STEP 1 In a large bowl, combine the balsamic vinegar, sherry vinegar and onion. Let stand at room temperature for 1 hour.

STEP 2 In another large bowl, cover the radicchio with ice water and let stand for 15 minutes. Drain and dry well.

STEP 3 Remove the onion from the vinegar; discard the onion. Whisk the honey and olive oil into the vinegar and add the radicchio and 1 cup of the Manchego. Season with salt and pepper and toss to coat evenly. Mound the radicchio on a platter, top with the remaining ½ cup of Manchego and serve.

WINE TIP Surprisingly, tart foods like vinaigrettes work best with equally tart wines–such as a crisp, unoaked Pinot Grigio.

Spicy Stir-Fried Cucumbers with Shredded Chicken

In China, cucumbers are a popular stir-fry ingredient because they remain tender, crisp and juicy in a sizzling wok. Slender, seedless cukes, like the Persian variety, are best here—they're less watery than other kinds.

TIME	MAKES	CONTRIBUTED BY
30 min total	**4 servings**	**Kay Chun**

12 oz. skinless, boneless chicken breast cutlets, pounded ⅛ inch thick and very thinly sliced crosswise

5 garlic cloves, smashed

1 Tbsp. finely chopped peeled fresh ginger

1 tsp. baking soda

Kosher salt and black pepper

¼ cup distilled white vinegar

1 tsp. sugar

3 Tbsp. canola oil

12 dried red chiles, such as chiles de árbol—10 left whole, 2 stemmed and crumbled

1 lb. seedless cucumbers, preferably Persian, cut into 1½-inch pieces

1 serrano chile, thinly sliced

¼ cup chopped cilantro sprigs

Lemon wedges and steamed rice, for serving

STEP 1 In a medium bowl, toss the chicken with half of the garlic and ginger and the baking soda; season with salt and pepper. In a small bowl, stir the vinegar with the sugar and ¼ cup of water.

STEP 2 In a large skillet, heat 2 tablespoons of the oil until shimmering. Add the chicken and stir-fry over moderately high heat until almost cooked through, about 2 minutes; transfer the chicken to a plate.

STEP 3 Add the remaining 1 tablespoon of oil to the skillet along with the whole and crumbled dried chiles, the cucumbers, vinegar mixture and the remaining garlic and ginger; season with salt and pepper. Stir-fry over moderate heat until the cucumbers are softened and most of the liquid has evaporated, about 3 minutes.

STEP 4 Add the chicken and serrano chile to the skillet and stir-fry until the chicken is cooked through, about 1 minute. Stir in the chopped cilantro and season with salt and pepper. Serve the stir-fry with lemon wedges and steamed rice.

Mixed Citrus & Arugula Salad

This salad calls for a trio of citrus, including fleshy, tangy navel oranges. Cookbook author Grace Parisi especially likes Cara Caras, a variety of navel orange with a lovely pink hue and delicate flavor. No matter what kind you choose, you'll get a big dose of vitamin C.

TIME **20 min total**	MAKES **4 servings**	CONTRIBUTED BY **Grace Parisi**

2 navel oranges

2 tangerines

3 clementines

1 large shallot, sliced paper-thin

3 Tbsp. chopped mint

1 Tbsp. fresh lime juice

1 Tbsp. walnut oil

1 Tbsp. crème fraîche or sour cream

2 bunches of arugula (¼ lb. each), tough stems discarded

Kosher salt and pepper

STEP 1 Using a sharp knife, peel the oranges, tangerines and clementines, removing all the bitter white pith. Slice the clementines crosswise ½ inch thick and remove any seeds. Transfer the clementines to a medium bowl. Working over the bowl, cut between the membranes of the oranges and tangerines, releasing the sections into the bowl. Add the shallot and mint.

STEP 2 In a large bowl, whisk the lime juice with the walnut oil and crème fraîche. Add the arugula, season with salt and pepper and toss gently. Using tongs, transfer the arugula to plates. Add the citrus fruits to the remaining dressing, season with salt and pepper and toss to coat. Top the arugula with the citrus and serve.

Prep Ahead
The salad can be prepared through Step 1 and refrigerated for up to 2 hours.

WINE TIP
For citrusy salads, choose a wine with similarly bright and fruity flavors, like an Italian Vermentino.

Spaghetti with Fresh Asparagus Pesto

Who says pesto has to be made with herbs alone? Using raw asparagus creates a very fresh, green and spring-like sauce to toss with pasta.

TIME **30 min total**	MAKES **4 servings**	CONTRIBUTED BY **Kay Chun**

¾ lb. spaghetti

1 lb. asparagus, trimmed and coarsely chopped

½ cup extra-virgin olive oil, plus more for drizzling

¼ cup freshly grated Parmigiano-Reggiano cheese

½ cup basil leaves, torn if large

1 Tbsp. fresh lemon juice

Kosher salt and pepper

STEP 1 In a large pot of salted boiling water, cook the pasta until al dente. Drain, reserving ¼ cup of the cooking water.

STEP 2 Meanwhile, in a food processor, pulse the asparagus until finely chopped. Transfer to a large bowl. Stir in the ½ cup of olive oil along with the cheese, basil and lemon juice. Season with salt and pepper. Add the hot pasta and reserved cooking water and toss until the pasta is well coated with pesto. Season with salt and pepper, drizzle with olive oil and serve.

Crispy Tofu Steaks with Ginger Vinaigrette

Crispy outside and creamy within, these fried tofu steaks will turn even the staunchest bean curd haters into fans.

TIME **30 min total**	MAKES **4 servings**	CONTRIBUTED BY **Kay Chun** 📷

3 Tbsp. minced peeled fresh ginger

3 Tbsp. minced scallion

1 Tbsp. distilled white vinegar

⅔ cup canola oil

Kosher salt

1 large egg

1 cup panko

One 14-oz. package firm tofu, drained and sliced 1 inch thick

STEP 1 In a small bowl, mix the ginger with the scallion, vinegar and ⅓ cup of the oil; season the vinaigrette with salt.

STEP 2 Beat the egg in a medium bowl. Spread the panko on a plate. Dip the tofu slices in the egg, then coat in the panko. In a large nonstick skillet, heat the remaining ⅓ cup of oil. Fry the tofu over moderate heat, turning, until golden and crispy, about 8 minutes. Season with salt and serve with the ginger vinaigrette.

Grilled Cucumbers & Eggplant

If you never thought to grill cucumbers, now's the time to try it. They're surprisingly delicious charred alongside eggplant and tossed with a garlicky anchovy vinaigrette.

TIME	MAKES	CONTRIBUTED BY
20 min total	**4 servings**	**Kay Chun**

¼ cup extra-virgin olive oil, plus more for brushing

¼ cup red wine vinegar

5 garlic cloves, minced

5 anchovy fillets, minced

Kosher salt and pepper

4 Persian or Kirby cucumbers, quartered lengthwise

1 small eggplant, halved lengthwise and cut into wedges

Leaves from 1 small bunch of basil

Crusty bread, for serving

STEP 1 Light a grill or heat a grill pan. In a large bowl, whisk the ¼ cup of oil with the vinegar, garlic and anchovies; season with salt and pepper. In another large bowl, toss the cucumbers and eggplant with 3 tablespoons of the vinaigrette.

STEP 2 Oil the grate and grill the vegetables over moderate heat, turning, until the cucumbers are crisp-tender and the eggplant is tender, 3 to 5 minutes. Transfer the vegetables to the bowl with the vinaigrette and add the basil; toss to coat. Serve warm, at room temperature or cold, with bread.

Scallop Carpaccio with Hand-Cut Ginger-Chive Pesto

Sliced thin and marinated, scallops are wonderful raw in carpaccios like the one here. Crunchy flakes of sea salt and crisp radish slices add terrific texture.

TIME	MAKES	CONTRIBUTED BY
25 min total	**4 servings**	**Kay Chun**

2 Tbsp. minced peeled fresh ginger

¼ cup finely chopped chives

¼ cup extra-virgin olive oil

1 Tbsp. fresh lime juice, plus lime wedges for serving

Kosher salt and pepper

½ lb. sea scallops, thinly sliced crosswise

Flaky sea salt and thinly sliced radishes, for garnish

STEP 1 In a small bowl, combine the ginger, chives, olive oil and lime juice; season with kosher salt and pepper and mix well.

STEP 2 Arrange the scallops on a platter and top with the ginger-chive pesto. Season with flaky sea salt and garnish with sliced radishes. Serve with lime wedges.

Crab Salad with Paprika–Scallion Mayonnaise

Linton Hopkins of Atlanta's Restaurant Eugene marinates lump crabmeat overnight to boost the flavor, then combines it with a scallion-and-paprika-spiked mayonnaise for this crowd-pleasing dip.

TIME **30 min, plus overnight marinating**	MAKES **8 servings**	CONTRIBUTED BY **Linton Hopkins**

1 cup finely chopped Vidalia or other sweet onion

1 lb. jumbo lump crabmeat

Kosher salt and pepper

½ cup peanut oil

½ cup ice water

⅓ cup plus 1 Tbsp. apple cider vinegar

¾ cup mayonnaise

1 Tbsp. fresh lemon juice

¼ tsp. sweet paprika

2 Tbsp. thinly sliced scallions

¼ cup coarsely chopped flat-leaf parsley

½ small red onion, thinly sliced, for garnish

Buttered toast points or saltines, for serving

STEP 1 Spread half of the chopped onion in a large bowl. Top with the crab, season with salt and pepper and cover with the remaining chopped onion. In a small bowl, whisk the oil with the ice water and ⅓ cup of the vinegar. Pour over the crab, cover and refrigerate overnight.

STEP 2 In a medium bowl, combine the mayonnaise with the lemon juice, paprika and the remaining 1 tablespoon of vinegar. Drain the crab and fold it into the mayonnaise along with the scallions and parsley. Garnish with the red onion and serve with toast points.

WINE TIP

Crab, like most other shellfish, tastes better with white wines that haven't been aged in oak. Pinot Grigio is a great example.

Spicy Fideos with Mussels & Calamari

This comforting Catalan dish is similar to paella, but instead of rice, it's made with short noodles called fideos. The pasta is first browned in oil, then simmered with just a bit of stock and lots of fresh seafood. Here, it's finished with parsley and crunchy marcona almonds.

TIME **50 min total**	MAKES **4 servings**	CONTRIBUTED BY **Kay Chun**

¼ cup chopped parsley

¼ cup chopped marcona almonds

2 Tbsp. extra-virgin olive oil

1 shallot, finely chopped

3 garlic cloves, minced

2 dried chiles de árbol, stemmed and crumbled

7 oz. fideos or angel hair pasta, broken into 1-inch lengths (2 cups)

Kosher salt and pepper

1 small tomato, diced

1 Tbsp. tomato paste

Pinch of saffron threads

1 cup chicken stock or low-sodium broth

One 8-oz. bottle clam juice

1 lb. mussels, scrubbed and debearded

½ lb. cleaned squid, bodies cut into ¼-inch-thick rings and tentacles left whole

STEP 1 In a small bowl, combine the parsley and almonds.

STEP 2 In a large enameled cast-iron casserole or paella pan, heat the oil. Add the shallot, garlic, chiles and fideos, season with salt and pepper and cook over moderately low heat, stirring occasionally, until the fideos are lightly toasted, about 5 minutes. Stir in the tomato, tomato paste and saffron and cook, stirring, until the tomato paste is lightly caramelized, about 3 minutes. Stir in the stock and clam juice and bring to a simmer. Cook over moderate heat until the fideos are al dente, about 5 minutes.

STEP 3 Stir the mussels and calamari into the casserole, cover and cook over low heat until the mussels open, 8 to 10 minutes. Discard any mussels that don't open. Season with salt and pepper, top with the parsley and almonds and serve.

WINE TIP Often it's effective to pair wines and foods from the same culture–so try a Spanish white like Godello with this dish.

Warm Seafood Salad with Pistachios & Capers

Cookbook author Jane Sigal adapted this recipe from one by chef Francesco Cutrì of Ciccio e Pinolo, in the Ligurian port city of La Spezia. The shrimp-and-squid salad gets its piquant kick from a dressing of capers, olive oil and ground pistachios.

TIME **30 min total**	MAKES **4 servings**	CONTRIBUTED BY **Jane Sigal**

2 anchovy fillets, coarsely chopped

1 Tbsp. coarsely chopped unsalted pistachios

1 Tbsp. capers, drained

1 garlic clove, coarsely chopped

¼ cup extra-virgin olive oil

1 Tbsp. fresh lemon juice

½ lb. medium shrimp—shelled, deveined and halved lengthwise

½ lb. cleaned squid, bodies cut into ¼-inch-thick rings and tentacles left whole

STEP 1 In a mortar, pound the anchovies with the pistachios, capers, garlic and 1 tablespoon of the olive oil until fairly smooth. Stir in the remaining 3 tablespoons of olive oil and the lemon juice.

STEP 2 Bring a medium saucepan of salted water to a boil. Add the shrimp and cook until just white throughout, about 20 seconds. Using a slotted spoon, transfer the shrimp to a medium bowl. Add the squid to the saucepan and cook until just firm, about 20 seconds. Drain the squid and transfer them to the bowl.

STEP 3 Add the pistachio dressing to the bowl with the seafood and toss to coat. Mound the salad on plates and serve.

Prep Ahead
The pistachio dressing can be made up to 4 hours ahead and kept at room temperature.

Serve With
Crusty bread.

Cod with Basque Wine Sauce

Janet Mendel, author of *My Kitchen in Spain,* cooks cod fillets in a white wine sauce inspired by her travels to the Spanish Basque region. She amps up the sauce with cockles and shrimp to give the dish an even brinier flavor.

TIME	MAKES	CONTRIBUTED BY
30 min total	**4 servings**	**Janet Mendel**

3 Tbsp. extra-virgin olive oil

Four 5-oz. skinless cod fillets, halved crosswise

Kosher salt and pepper

2 Tbsp. all-purpose flour

3 large garlic cloves, thinly sliced

¾ cup frozen peas

⅓ cup finely chopped flat-leaf parsley

½ cup dry white wine

1 lb. cockles, rinsed

6 oz. shelled and deveined medium shrimp

In a large nonstick skillet, heat the olive oil until shimmering. Season the fish with salt and pepper and dust all over with 1 tablespoon of the flour. Add the fish and garlic to the skillet and cook over moderately high heat until barely golden, about 2 minutes. Sprinkle the remaining 1 tablespoon of flour over the fish. Turn the fish and add the peas, half of the parsley, the wine and the cockles. Cook, shaking the skillet occasionally, until the cod is almost cooked, about 4 minutes. Add the shrimp, tucking them into the liquid. Cover and cook for 2 to 3 minutes, until the shrimp are pink and curled and the cockles have opened. Discard any unopened cockles. Sprinkle with the remaining parsley and serve in shallow bowls.

WINE TIP

A good, inexpensive Pinot Grigio can be used *in* this dish as well as served alongside it.

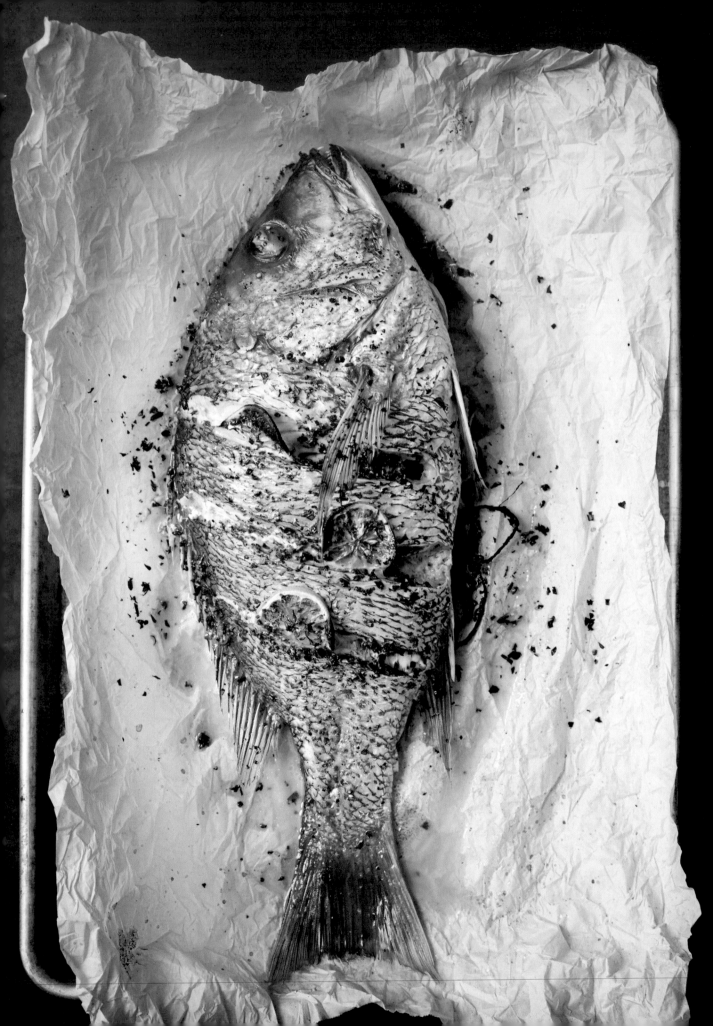

Whole Roast Fish with Lemon & Herbs

Athena Calderone, the designer and blogger behind EyeSwoon, loves to serve whole fish at dinner parties. "It looks really beautiful and dramatic, especially this colorful red snapper with blistered skin," she says. A vivid green salsa verde keeps the flavors bright and makes the dish even more visually striking.

TIME	MAKES	CONTRIBUTED BY
30 min active; 50 min total	**4 servings**	**Athena Calderone**

FISH

One 2½-lb. whole fish, such as red snapper, cleaned and scaled

2 Tbsp. extra-virgin olive oil

Kosher salt and pepper

1 lemon, thinly sliced

¼ cup chopped mixed herbs, such as thyme, oregano, parsley and rosemary

1 shallot, thinly sliced

¼ fennel bulb, thinly sliced

3 garlic cloves, crushed

SALSA VERDE

½ cup minced parsley

¼ cup minced basil

¼ cup minced mint

1 Tbsp. minced capers

1 tsp. red wine vinegar

1 garlic clove, minced

½ jalapeño (optional)

1 cup extra-virgin olive oil

2 Tbsp. fresh lemon juice

Kosher salt and pepper

STEP 1 MAKE THE FISH Preheat the oven to 450°. Put the fish on a parchment paper–lined baking sheet. Make 3 crosswise slashes down to the bone on each side of the fish. Rub with the olive oil and season with salt and pepper. Stuff each slash with 1 lemon slice and some herbs. Stuff the cavity with the shallot, fennel, garlic and remaining lemon slices and herbs. Roast for about 20 minutes, until the flesh is opaque.

STEP 2 MAKE THE SALSA VERDE In a medium bowl, mix all of the ingredients. Serve the fish with the salsa verde.

Prep Ahead
The salsa verde can be refrigerated overnight.

WINE **TIP**

Light seafood dishes seem to take on more flavor when matched with equally delicate white wines, such as Pinot Grigio or Arneis from Italy or French Chablis.

Grape Leaf–Wrapped Salmon with Serrano–Scallion Sauce

Chefs use all sorts of wraps for roasting fish, from sheets of seaweed to banana leaves. There are two benefits—the fish takes on the delicate flavor of the wrap, which also traps in moisture, so the fillets come out of the oven fantastically moist. The brined, jarred grape leaves used here are available at specialty markets and from amazon.com.

TIME **45 min total**	MAKES **4 servings**	CONTRIBUTED BY **Justin Chapple**

16 large jarred grape leaves, drained and patted dry

1 cup orange or yellow grape tomatoes, halved

5 scallions, julienned, plus 2 Tbsp. minced scallion

3 serrano chiles with seeds, halved and thinly sliced

Kosher salt and pepper

Four 6-oz. skinless salmon fillets

2 Tbsp. unsalted butter

¼ cup Champagne vinegar

½ cup heavy cream

STEP 1 Preheat the oven to 450° and line a large rimmed baking sheet with parchment paper. Arrange the grape leaves in groups of 4 on a work surface, overlapping them slightly. Mound the tomatoes, three-fourths of the julienned scallions and one-third of the sliced serranos in the center of the grape leaves and season lightly with salt and pepper. Season the salmon fillets with salt and pepper and place them on top, then wrap the grape leaves around the fish. Carefully turn the packets seam side down on the prepared baking sheet and roast for 10 to 12 minutes, until the salmon is medium within. Transfer the packets to plates.

STEP 2 Meanwhile, in a small saucepan, melt the butter. Add the minced scallion and cook over moderate heat, stirring, until softened, about 2 minutes. Add the vinegar and bring to a boil. Simmer over moderately high heat until reduced by half, about 3 minutes. Whisk in the cream and bring just to a simmer, then cook over moderately high heat, whisking occasionally, until slightly thickened, about 2 minutes. Stir in the remaining serranos and season the sauce with salt and pepper.

STEP 3 Cut open the salmon packets and drizzle the sauce over the fish. Garnish with the remaining julienned scallions and serve right away.

Beer–Steamed Shrimp with Cocktail Sauce

L.A. chef Suzanne Goin serves these well-spiced peel-and-eat shrimp at The Backyard restaurant at the Hollywood Bowl. The recipe comes from her husband, chef David Lentz, who's been cooking the dish for his family for years. It's easily scaled up to serve more people, which makes it ideal for parties.

TIME **40 min total**	MAKES **4 servings**	CONTRIBUTED BY **Suzanne Goin**

1½ lbs. extra-large shrimp

3 Tbsp. extra-virgin olive oil

1 onion, halved and thinly sliced

1 head of garlic, halved crosswise

1 rosemary sprig

1 chile de árbol, crushed

One 12-oz. can of beer, preferably Pabst Blue Ribbon

2 lemons, halved

2 Tbsp. Old Bay Seasoning

½ cup ketchup

1 Tbsp. drained prepared horseradish

2¼ tsp. fresh lemon juice

1½ tsp. Sriracha

¾ tsp. Worcestershire sauce

STEP 1 Using kitchen shears, cut along the back of each shrimp shell and remove the intestinal vein. In a large saucepan, heat the olive oil. Add the onion, garlic, rosemary and chile and cook over moderately high heat, stirring occasionally, until the onion is softened and just starting to brown, 5 to 7 minutes. Add the beer and simmer until reduced by half, about 5 minutes.

STEP 2 Add the lemon halves, Old Bay and 5 cups of water to the saucepan and bring just to a simmer. Add the shrimp and poach over low heat until just cooked through, 8 to 10 minutes. Using a slotted spoon, transfer the shrimp, onion, garlic and lemon halves to a platter to cool slightly.

STEP 3 Meanwhile, in a medium bowl, whisk the ketchup with the horseradish, lemon juice, Sriracha and Worcestershire.

STEP 4 Serve the shrimp, warm or at room temperature, with the cocktail sauce.

Prep Ahead

The cocktail sauce can be refrigerated for up to 5 days.

Halibut in Parchment with Corn & Tomatoes

Top Chef Season 10 winner Kristen Kish creates a simple, all-in-one meal by roasting halibut, corn, tomatoes and green beans in parchment. The upside to cooking this way: The aroma and juices of the fish stay contained in the packet, which puffs up with steam as it bakes, allowing the flavors of the herbs and spices to mingle.

TIME	MAKES	CONTRIBUTED BY
20 min active; 1 hr total	**4 servings**	**Kristen Kish**

One 1½-lb. center-cut skinless halibut fillet (1 inch thick)

1 Tbsp. sugar

2 tsp. fennel seeds

1 tsp. whole black peppercorns, plus ground pepper for seasoning

1 tsp. whole coriander seeds

Kosher salt

4 ears of corn, kernels cut off 3, 1 cob reserved

6 oz. wax or green beans, trimmed (2 cups)

15 small cherry tomatoes (about 8 oz.), preferably on the vine

2 Tbsp. extra-virgin olive oil

½ Tbsp. white wine vinegar

3 tarragon sprigs

2 thyme sprigs

4 Tbsp. unsalted butter, cubed

STEP 1 Place the halibut in a shallow baking dish. In a medium saucepan, combine 1 cup of water with the sugar, fennel seeds, peppercorns, coriander seeds and 2½ tablespoons of kosher salt and bring to a simmer. Cook, stirring, until the salt and sugar dissolve. Remove the pan from the heat and stir in 3 cups of ice water. Pour the cold brine over the halibut and let stand at room temperature for 25 minutes. Remove the halibut from the brine and pat dry; discard the brine. Season the halibut lightly on one side with salt and pepper.

STEP 2 Preheat the oven to 400°. Arrange a 12-by-32-inch piece of parchment paper on a baking sheet. Mound the corn kernels on one half of the parchment paper and top with the fish, skinless side up, leaving a 3-inch border on 3 sides. Top with the beans and tomatoes, then drizzle with the oil and vinegar. Scatter the tarragon and thyme on top. Set the reserved corn cob next to the fish. Top the fish with the butter.

Fold the parchment over the fish and pleat, fold and crimp the edges to seal; add 3 tablespoons of water before completely sealing the packet.

STEP 3 Roast the packet for 20 minutes, until the halibut is just opaque throughout. Transfer the packet to a serving platter, open and serve.

Potted Ham with Cabbage & Pickles

This easy spread is an excellent make-ahead party dish that can sit out for a few hours and still taste great.

TIME	MAKES	CONTRIBUTED BY
20 min total	**2 cups**	**Kay Chun**

2 oil-packed anchovy fillets

¼ cup extra-virgin olive oil

½ lb. smoked ham, shredded

1 cup finely chopped green cabbage

1 small dill pickle, chopped (⅓ cup)

2 Tbsp. chopped dill, plus more for garnish

Kosher salt and pepper

In a small saucepan, melt the anchovies in the olive oil over moderate heat, stirring. Scrape the anchovy oil into a medium bowl. Add the ham, cabbage, pickle and chopped dill; season with salt and pepper and mix well. Pack the ham mixture into a 3-cup ramekin and garnish with dill. Serve at room temperature.

Serve With
Toasted country bread and mustard.

Bacon-Wrapped Vegetable Skewers with Dill Pickle Relish

Ordinary pickles can be deployed as powerful flavor bombs — they're used here both as a seasoning and in a dipping sauce for smoky grilled oyster mushrooms and cherry tomatoes.

TIME	MAKES	CONTRIBUTED BY
40 min total	**10 servings**	**Paul Berglund**

¾ cup minced dill pickles

¾ cup minced parsley

¾ cup extra-virgin olive oil, plus more for brushing

Kosher salt

¾ lb. oyster mushrooms, sliced and arranged in 2-inch clusters

20 large cherry tomatoes

20 thin strips of bacon (1 lb.), halved crosswise

Lemon wedges, for serving

STEP 1 In a bowl, toss the pickles, parsley and the ¾ cup of olive oil. Season the relish with salt.

STEP 2 Light a grill. Wrap each mushroom cluster and cherry tomato in a bacon slice. Thread the bacon-wrapped vegetables onto skewers. Brush with olive oil and season lightly with salt. Grill the skewers over moderate heat, turning, until the bacon is cooked and the vegetables are tender, about 8 minutes; brush with a little pickle relish during the last minute of grilling. Transfer to a platter and serve with lemon wedges and the remaining pickle relish.

SAUVIGNON BLANC
& OTHER TART, CITRUSY WHITES

SAUVIGNON BLANC The wide flavor spectrum of Sauvignon Blanc may well elicit the most exotic and diverse tasting notes of any grape on the planet—from gooseberry to green pepper to grapefruit to passion fruit to green beans. That every region coaxes a different personality from the grape makes the character of Sauvignon Blanc a little tricky to pinpoint; it can be a love-it-or-hate-it proposition. A quick scan of wine shop shelves usually reveals dozens of Sauvignon Blanc choices, pointing to the fact that the grape is grown just about everywhere—from Bordeaux to New Zealand to California to Chile. To really get a grip on this mutable variety, try tasting a few examples.

In France, the grape's native home, two regions are best known for Sauvignon: Bordeaux and the Loire Valley. In Bordeaux, Sauvignons are often blended with Sémillon and aged in oak barrels; they tend to be rounder and more restrained, versus the zesty, minerally wines of the Loire's Sancerre and Pouilly-Fumé subregions. Sauvignons from California show off the state's intense sunshine with ripe tropical-fruit aromas and more substantial body. The same is true of bottles from South Africa's Stellenbosch region. New Zealand has made a name for itself with its own genre of Sauvignon Blanc, wines that often have a distinct green pepper aroma matched by juicy citrus fruit. Sauvignons from Chile tend to be fragrant and lemony; they're deserving of more attention than they usually receive.

No matter where they're from, the wines are generally medium-bodied, with lively acidity, making them a great match for seafood and vegetable-based dishes—anything you'd squeeze a lemon on.

ALBARIÑO & VERDEJO Spain's fame with red wines often means that its impressive whites are overlooked. That's a pity. Albariño, which comes from Galicia, in the northwest corner of the country, possesses a vibrancy and saltiness that make it a sublime pairing for the fresh seafood the area is so well-known for. Top winemakers in Galicia work with grapes from old vineyards, close to the coast, making for fantastically zesty, concentrated wines.

While it doesn't get anywhere near the appreciation that Albariño does, Verdejo, a white variety grown primarily in the rocky, dry, central region of Rueda, deserves recognition, too. Verdejos fall more on the green apple and juicy melon side of the flavor scale. Crisp and medium-bodied, they're a good match for grilled fish, chicken and salads, and can be great on their own, too—they're ideal party wines, nicely bridging the gap between Sauvignon Blanc and Chardonnay.

GRÜNER VELTLINER Make this vibrant Austrian white your go-to for vegetables that classically don't play all that well with wine. Grüner Veltliner (GROO-ner velt-LEE-ner) is unrivaled in its ability to pair with green vegetables (asparagus, artichokes, green peas, arugula) thanks to its savory, lemony and often peppery notes. Most of the world's Grüner Veltliner is grown in Austria, with the Wachau, Kremstal and Kamptal regions turning out the best renditions. It accounts for nearly 30 percent of the country's overall grape production. At the same time, a growing number of producers in California and New York are trying their hand with the grape, with intriguing results.

Known for impressive acidity and relatively low alcohol, Austrian Grüner (that's what the cool kids call it) comes in a variety of styles, from leaner and light-bodied to more ripe, with concentrated fruit. Less-expensive bottlings offer straightforward, citrusy freshness—they're quintessential summer whites, great with a salad—whereas the complexity and minerality of pricier, single-vineyard wines make them suitable for main courses like roast chicken or Austria's signature Wiener schnitzel.

Chile Oil–Marinated Goat Cheese

At the charming Les Arcades restaurant in the tiny town of Biot, some 15 miles from Nice, servers set out bowls of this marinated goat cheese so guests can help themselves. If you like, you can add a few sprigs of herbs, such as thyme or rosemary, to the olive oil along with the dried chiles. No matter how you flavor it, be sure to have plenty of crusty bread on hand to dip into the delicious oil.

TIME **10 min, plus 3 days marinating**	MAKES **6 servings**	ADAPTED FROM **Les Arcades, Biot, France**

9 dried chiles de árbol

One 11-oz. log of semifirm goat cheese, cut into 6 pieces

3 to 4 cups extra-virgin olive oil

Toasted sliced baguette or sourdough bread, for serving

Scatter 3 of the chiles in the bottom of a small bowl at least 3 inches deep. Arrange the cheese in a single layer over the chiles; top with 3 more chiles. Pour in enough oil to submerge the cheese. Crumble the remaining 3 chiles into the oil. Cover and marinate in the refrigerator for at least 3 days. Bring to room temperature before serving with bread. (Once the cheese is done, strain the chile oil and use in other dishes.)

Make Ahead
The cheese can be refrigerated for up to 1 week.

WINE TIP

The tanginess of goat cheese makes it a classic pairing with the tart herbaceousness of Sauvignon Blanc.

Pork–Kimchi Dumpling Pancakes

Corey Lee, the chef at Benu in San Francisco, ingeniously reinvents pan-fried pork-and-kimchi dumplings by adding a thin layer of batter that turns them into one round, lacy-crisp pancake. He serves it with a simple soy-and-vinegar dipping sauce that's spiked with *gochugaru* (Korean chile flakes), which you can find at Asian markets or online from amazon.com.

TIME	MAKES	CONTRIBUTED BY
1 hr total	**6 to 8 servings**	**Corey Lee**

DIPPING SAUCE

¼ cup soy sauce

1 Tbsp. white vinegar

1 Tbsp. sesame seeds

1 Tbsp. sugar

½ Tbsp. *gochugaru* (Korean red pepper flakes) or ½ Tbsp. crushed red pepper

DUMPLINGS

10 oz. ground pork

⅓ cup finely chopped drained kimchi

¼ cup firm tofu, finely chopped

2 scallions, minced

2 garlic cloves, minced

1 Tbsp. minced peeled fresh ginger

1 large egg, lightly beaten

1 Tbsp. soy sauce

1 tsp. kosher salt

30 gyoza wrappers

1½ Tbsp. cornstarch

3 Tbsp. canola oil

STEP 1 MAKE THE DIPPING SAUCE
In a small bowl, mix all of the ingredients until the sugar dissolves.

STEP 2 MAKE THE DUMPLINGS
In a large bowl, mix all of the ingredients except the wrappers, cornstarch and canola oil. Arrange 4 wrappers on a work surface; keep the rest covered with a damp paper towel. Brush the edges of the wrappers with water and drop 1 tablespoon of the pork filling in the centers. Fold over one side of each wrapper to form a half-moon, pressing the edges together. Transfer the dumplings to a parchment-lined baking sheet and cover with plastic wrap; assemble the remaining dumplings.

STEP 3 In a small bowl, stir the cornstarch with 1 cup plus 2 tablespoons of water to make a slurry.

STEP 4 Heat 1 tablespoon of the oil in an 8-inch nonstick skillet. Arrange 10 dumplings around the edge of the skillet, overlapping them slightly (there should be almost no empty space). Cook over moderate heat until golden on the bottom. Drizzle one-third of the slurry over and around the dumplings, cover the skillet and cook for 1 minute. Uncover and cook until the dumplings are cooked through and the slurry forms a thin crust, about 4 minutes. Carefully invert the dumpling pancake onto a plate. Repeat to make 2 more pancakes. Serve them with the dipping sauce.

Prep Ahead

The uncooked dumplings can be refrigerated for 4 hours or frozen for up to 1 month; allow additional cooking time if starting with frozen dumplings.

Goat Cheese, Bacon & Olive Quick Bread

Quick breads like this cheesy loaf from Paris-based cookbook author David Lebovitz are very popular in France, where they're known as *cakes salés* (savory cakes) and served with wine. This one, packed with kalamata olives, cheese and bacon, is infused with cayenne.

TIME **35 min active; 1 hr 15 min total, plus cooling**	MAKES **One 9-inch loaf**	CONTRIBUTED BY **David Lebovitz**

Nonstick cooking spray

6 slices of thick-cut bacon, cut crosswise into ½-inch-wide strips

1½ cups all-purpose flour

2 tsp. baking powder

1 to 2 tsp. cayenne

¼ tsp. kosher salt

4 large eggs, at room temperature

½ cup buttermilk

¼ cup extra-virgin olive oil

2 tsp. Dijon mustard

6 oz. fresh goat cheese, crumbled

1⅓ cups freshly grated Parmigiano-Reggiano cheese

½ cup pitted kalamata olives, halved lengthwise

2 scallions, thinly sliced

1 red serrano chile, seeded and minced

2 tsp. minced thyme

STEP 1 Preheat the oven to 350°. Coat a 9-inch loaf pan with cooking spray; line the bottom with parchment paper. In a skillet, cook the bacon over moderate heat until crispy, 8 to 10 minutes. Drain on paper towels.

STEP 2 In a large bowl, whisk the flour with the baking powder, cayenne and salt. In a medium bowl, whisk the eggs with the buttermilk, olive oil and mustard. Make a well in the center of the dry ingredients and stir in the egg mixture until just combined. Fold in the goat cheese, Parmigiano, olives, bacon, scallions, chile and thyme. Scrape the batter into the prepared loaf pan and smooth the surface.

STEP 3 Bake the bread until golden on top and a toothpick inserted in the center comes out clean, 35 to 40 minutes. Let cool for 15 minutes, then run a knife around the loaf to loosen it from the pan. Invert the loaf onto a plate and let cool completely. Cut into thick slices and serve.

Make Ahead
The bread can be wrapped well in plastic and refrigerated for up to 1 week.

Roasted Artichokes & Prosciutto

Artichokes are notorious for making wine taste sweet. To prevent that, California chef Michael Chiarello slow-roasts artichoke hearts in extra-virgin olive oil to bring out their sweetness, then serves them with prosciutto, an ingredient that matches particularly well with wine.

WINE TIP

Spring vegetables such as artichokes and asparagus can be tricky to pair with because they can make wine taste oddly sweet or even metallic. One wine that always works well is a citrusy Sauvignon Blanc.

TIME	MAKES	CONTRIBUTED BY
35 min active; 1 hr 30 min total	**8 servings**	**Michael Chiarello**

1 lemon, halved, plus 3 Tbsp. fresh lemon juice

6 large artichokes

⅔ cup extra-virgin olive oil

3 garlic cloves, quartered

1 tsp. coarsely chopped thyme

1 bay leaf

1 Tbsp. very finely chopped flat-leaf parsley

Kosher salt and pepper

½ lb. thinly sliced prosciutto

Crusty bread or bread sticks, for serving

STEP 1 Preheat the oven to 325°. Squeeze some of the juice from the lemon halves into a large bowl of water. Working with 1 artichoke at a time, snap off the dark green outer leaves. Slice off all but 1 inch of the remaining leaves. Peel and trim the bottom and stem of the artichoke. Halve the artichoke and scoop out the furry choke with a spoon. Cut the artichoke halves in half again, rub with the lemon and add the artichoke to the lemon water. Repeat with the remaining artichokes. Add the lemon halves to the water.

STEP 2 In a large ovenproof skillet, combine the 3 tablespoons of lemon juice with the olive oil, garlic, thyme and bay leaf. Drain the artichokes and add them to the skillet. Bring to a simmer over moderate heat, stirring occasionally.

STEP 3 Transfer the skillet to the oven and roast the artichokes for about 40 minutes, stirring a few times, until they are tender and browned in spots. Discard the bay leaf. Stir in the parsley and season with salt and pepper. Let cool.

STEP 4 Arrange the prosciutto slices on a platter. Spoon the artichokes and their cooking liquid into a bowl and serve with bread and the prosciutto.

Prep Ahead
The artichokes can be prepared through Step 3 and refrigerated overnight. Let come to room temperature before serving.

Quick Korean Egg Custards with Shrimp

Judy Joo, host of the Cooking Channel's *Korean Food Made Simple,* puts her own spin on the silky Korean egg custard called *gyeran jjim.* Traditionally, the dish is seasoned with tiny salted shrimp, but Joo tops hers with larger fresh shrimp and sesame seeds and oil.

TIME	MAKES	CONTRIBUTED BY
20 min total	**4 servings**	**Judy Joo**

8 large eggs

2 cups chicken stock or low-sodium broth

2 tsp. Asian fish sauce

½ tsp. kosher salt

8 small shelled and deveined shrimp (5 oz.)

1 scallion, thinly sliced

Toasted sesame seeds and toasted sesame oil, for garnish

STEP 1 In a large bowl, whisk the eggs with the stock, fish sauce and salt. Pour the mixture into four 10-ounce heatproof bowls or ramekins. Arrange the bowls in 2 large, wide pots with lids. Add enough boiling water to the pots to reach two-thirds of the way up the sides of the bowls. Bring the water to a simmer, cover and simmer gently until the custards are slightly wobbly in the centers, 6 to 7 minutes.

STEP 2 Divide the shrimp and scallion among the bowls, cover and steam until the shrimp are cooked through and the custards are set, 3 minutes longer. Garnish the custards with sesame seeds and sesame oil; serve warm.

WINE TIP Eggs or eggy custards tend to coat your mouth—a tart, high-acid white like Spanish Albariño cuts right through that.

Green Pea Samosas (Hare Mutter Ki Samosa)

WINE TIP

Austrian Grüner Veltliner is known for its light pea-shoot character–which also makes it a fine match for green peas.

Indian chef Sanjeev Chopra has this advice for filling his delightful vegetarian samosas: "Mash the peas, but not too finely; you want little pieces, for texture." He makes his own buttery dough, but frozen empanada wrappers, widely available in supermarkets, are an excellent substitute.

TIME **45 min total**	MAKES **8 samosas**	CONTRIBUTED BY **Sanjeev Chopra**

1 Tbsp. canola oil, plus more for frying

¼ tsp. cumin seeds

1 tsp. minced peeled fresh ginger

1 tsp. minced seeded jalapeño

½ tsp. ground coriander

¼ tsp. cayenne

1 lb. frozen green peas, thawed

1 Tbsp. chopped cilantro

1 tsp. pomegranate molasses (optional)

Kosher salt

8 frozen empanada wrappers, thawed

Prepared cilantro chutney and tamarind chutney, for serving

STEP 1 In a medium skillet, heat the 1 tablespoon of oil. Add the cumin seeds and cook over moderate heat until fragrant, about 30 seconds. Add the ginger, jalapeño, coriander and cayenne and cook, stirring, until fragrant, about 30 seconds more. Add the peas and ½ cup of water and cook until the peas are tender and most of the water has evaporated, about 5 minutes. Transfer the mixture to a food processor and let cool slightly. Add the cilantro and pomegranate molasses, if using, and pulse until the peas are finely chopped. Season with salt.

STEP 2 Arrange the empanada wrappers on a work surface and brush the edges with water. Divide the filling among the wrappers. Fold each dough round over to form a cone and pinch from the tip of the cone along the seam. Fold the top of the dough down to meet the edges and pinch well to seal, forming a triangular dumpling.

STEP 3 In a deep, medium skillet, heat ¾ inch of oil to 350°. Fry the samosas over moderately high heat, turning once, until golden and crisp, about 5 minutes. Drain on a paper towel–lined rack. Serve the samosas with cilantro and tamarind chutneys.

Spaghetti with Clams and Braised Greens

Ashley Christensen of Poole's Downtown Diner in Raleigh, North Carolina, adds a secret ingredient to her clam sauce: pureed roasted red bell peppers. They not only give the spicy, briny broth great flavor and color, "the roasted peppers really help the sauce 'hug' the pasta," she says.

TIME **45 min total**	MAKES **4 servings**	CONTRIBUTED BY **Ashley Christensen**

½ cup extra-virgin olive oil

8 garlic cloves, crushed

4 dozen littleneck clams

2 cups dry white wine

2 jarred roasted red peppers, drained

1 tsp. crushed red pepper

1 lb. Swiss chard or collard greens, stemmed and chopped (8 cups)

Kosher salt and black pepper

½ lb. spaghetti

2 Tbsp. unsalted butter, cubed and chilled

1 tsp. finely grated lemon zest plus 1 Tbsp. fresh lemon juice

½ cup freshly grated Parmigiano-Reggiano cheese, plus more for garnish

STEP 1 In a large pot, heat ¼ cup of the oil. Add half of the garlic and cook over moderate heat, stirring, for 1 minute. Stir in the clams. Add the wine and bring to a boil. Cover and cook over moderately high heat, stirring occasionally, for 5 to 7 minutes; as the clams open, transfer them to a baking sheet. Discard any unopened clams. Strain the cooking liquid through a sieve into a blender. Add the roasted peppers; puree until smooth.

STEP 2 Wash out the pot, then heat the remaining ¼ cup of oil in it. Add the remaining garlic and cook over moderate heat, stirring, for 1 minute. Stir in the crushed red pepper and Swiss chard in batches until the chard is just wilted, about 3 minutes. Stir in the roasted pepper broth and season with salt and black pepper.

STEP 3 In a large pot of salted boiling water, cook the spaghetti until al dente; drain. Add the pasta to the Swiss chard mixture along with the butter, lemon zest, lemon juice and the ½ cup of grated cheese. Add the clams and toss to heat through. Transfer the pasta, clams and broth to shallow bowls, garnish with grated cheese and serve.

Spaghetti with Radish Greens Pesto

The next time you buy radishes, save the tops. The brightly flavored greens have some bite, but they're milder than you might expect. Add them to salads, soups, salsa verde or anywhere you want a lightly pungent hit of flavor. This vibrant pesto variation is more peppery than the traditional one made with basil. You can also use beet or turnip tops or any assertive leaves, such as watercress, arugula or mustard greens.

TIME **30 min total**	MAKES **4 servings**	CONTRIBUTED BY **Kay Chun**

2 garlic cloves, crushed

Greens from 1 big bunch of radishes (8 loosely packed cups), chopped

¼ cup parsley leaves

¾ cup roasted salted pumpkin seeds (3 oz.), plus more for garnish

¾ cup extra-virgin olive oil

1 cup freshly grated Parmigiano-Reggiano cheese, plus more for garnish

Kosher salt and pepper

¾ lb. spaghetti

2 Tbsp. fresh lemon juice

STEP 1 In a food processor, combine the garlic, greens, parsley leaves and the ¾ cup of pumpkin seeds; pulse until finely chopped. With the machine on, slowly drizzle in the olive oil. Stir in the 1 cup of cheese. Season the pesto with salt and pepper.

STEP 2 In a pot of salted boiling water, cook the spaghetti until al dente. Drain, reserving 1 cup of the pasta water. Return the pasta to the pot. Add the pesto, lemon juice and ½ cup of the pasta water. Season with salt and pepper and toss over low heat until coated, about 2 minutes; add more pasta water if a thinner consistency is desired.

STEP 3 Transfer the pasta to bowls, garnish with pumpkin seeds and cheese and serve.

WINE TIP Pesto and other green, herbal sauces can pair very well with wines that offer a similar herbaceousness, like Sauvignon Blanc.

Chickpea–Vegetable Stew

"Talk about Meatless Monday!" says Cathal Armstrong, chef at Restaurant Eve in Alexandria, Virginia. "This is a great one-pot dish that I cooked for the CEO of Whole Foods." It's since become a quick weeknight go-to for Armstrong's family. He gives the stew heft with fingerling potatoes and chickpeas, creaminess with coconut milk and subtle heat with harissa.

TIME	MAKES	CONTRIBUTED BY
35 min total	**4 servings**	**Cathal Armstrong**

2 Tbsp. olive oil

1 cup pearl onions—blanched, peeled (or thawed frozen) and halved

1 red bell pepper, diced

½ lb. fingerling potatoes, halved lengthwise

2 garlic cloves, minced

1 Tbsp. finely chopped peeled fresh ginger

1 Tbsp. harissa (North African chile paste)

3 cups chicken stock or low sodium broth

One 15-oz. can chickpeas, drained and rinsed

¾ cup unsweetened coconut milk

2 Tbsp. fresh lemon juice

Kosher salt and pepper

1 Tbsp. minced cilantro

Toasted flatbread, for serving

STEP 1 In a large saucepan, heat the olive oil. Add the onions and bell pepper and cook over moderately high heat, stirring, until browned, about 5 minutes. Add the potatoes, garlic, ginger and harissa and cook, stirring, until the harissa darkens, about 2 minutes. Add the chicken stock and chickpeas and bring to a boil. Cover and simmer over moderately low heat until the potatoes are tender, 12 to 14 minutes.

STEP 2 Add the coconut milk to the pan and bring to a simmer. Stir in the lemon juice and season with salt and pepper. Sprinkle the stew with the cilantro and serve with toasted bread.

WINE TIP

The creamy richness of coconut milk can be *too* rich unless you counter it with a zingy, tart wine like Italian Arneis or Spanish Albariño.

Cauliflower Steaks with Herb Salsa Verde

"I can fool my family into thinking we're eating a meaty meal with this dish," says chef Alex Guarnaschelli of Butter in New York City. "And they're a tough crowd." She treats thick slices of cauliflower like steaks, searing and topping them with a super-tangy salsa verde whisked with Dijon mustard. The salsa would also be fabulous on beef steaks and other roasted or grilled vegetables.

| TIME
35 min total | MAKES
2 to 4 servings | CONTRIBUTED BY
Alex Guarnaschelli |

¼ cup chopped flat-leaf parsley

2 Tbsp. chopped cilantro

2 Tbsp. chopped tarragon

1½ Tbsp. capers, drained and coarsely chopped

6 cornichons, chopped

1 small garlic clove, minced

1 Tbsp. Dijon mustard

1 Tbsp. grainy mustard

⅓ cup extra-virgin olive oil

1 large head of cauliflower

Kosher salt and pepper

2 Tbsp. canola oil

½ cup dry white wine

½ tsp. finely grated lemon zest plus 4½ Tbsp. fresh lemon juice

1 tsp. red wine vinegar

STEP 1 In a large bowl, whisk the parsley with the cilantro, tarragon, capers, cornichons, garlic, mustards and olive oil.

STEP 2 Cut the cauliflower from top to bottom into four ½-inch-thick steaks. Generously season them with salt and pepper. In a very large skillet, heat the canola oil until very hot. Add the cauliflower steaks in a single layer and cook over high heat until browned, 2 to 3 minutes. Carefully turn the steaks, add the wine and cook until it is evaporated and the cauliflower is easily pierced with a knife, 3 to 5 minutes.

STEP 3 Transfer the cauliflower to a platter and sprinkle with the lemon zest. Stir the lemon juice and vinegar into the salsa verde and season with salt and pepper. Spoon the sauce on the cauliflower steaks and serve.

Prep Ahead

The salsa verde can be prepared through Step 1 and refrigerated overnight. Bring to room temperature before continuing.

Trout with Preserved Lemon Vinaigrette

This incredibly delicious pan-seared fish is a homey version of a dish that chef Viet Pham served at (the now-shuttered) Ember + Ash in Salt Lake City. He whisks bits of preserved lemon peel into the vinaigrette, giving a Moroccan flair to Utah's rainbow trout.

TIME	MAKES	CONTRIBUTED BY
30 min total	**6 servings**	**Viet Pham**

3 Tbsp. cider vinegar

2 Tbsp. fresh lemon juice

2 Tbsp. minced preserved lemon peel

1 Tbsp. minced shallot

1½ tsp. Asian fish sauce

1 tsp. sugar

½ cup grapeseed oil

1 Tbsp. finely chopped parsley

Kosher salt and pepper

Six 6-oz. trout fillets

2 cups watercress sprigs

STEP 1 In a medium bowl, whisk the vinegar, lemon juice, preserved lemon, minced shallot, fish sauce and sugar. Whisk in ¼ cup of the oil. Stir in the chopped parsley and season the vinaigrette with salt and pepper.

STEP 2 Season the trout with salt and pepper. In a large skillet, heat 2 tablespoons of the oil until shimmering. Add 3 trout fillets skin side down and press them with a spatula to flatten. Cook over high heat until the skin is crisp, about 3 minutes. Flip the fillets and cook until the fish is just white throughout, about 30 seconds; drain on paper towels. Wipe out the skillet. Repeat with the remaining 2 tablespoons of oil and 3 trout fillets.

STEP 3 Set the trout on plates, skin side up, and top with the watercress. Spoon some of the vinaigrette over the fish and watercress. Pass the remaining vinaigrette at the table.

WINE TIP Often cooked with a citrusy sauce, trout is terrific with a citrusy wine like a New Zealand Sauvignon Blanc.

Arctic Char with Charmoula

Jessica Koslow, chef at Sqirl in Los Angeles, puts her own spin on *charmoula*—a classic North African sauce packed with fresh herbs and spices—by adding toasted garlic. Her super-flavorful version is excellent with a rich fish, such as arctic char or salmon.

TIME **40 min total**	MAKES **4 servings**	CONTRIBUTED BY **Jessica Koslow**

3 unpeeled garlic cloves

⅓ cup plus 2 Tbsp. extra-virgin olive oil

¼ cup flat-leaf parsley leaves

¼ cup cilantro leaves

2 Tbsp. chopped green olives

1 Tbsp. fresh lemon juice

¼ tsp. ground cumin

¼ tsp. paprika

Kosher salt and pepper

Four 5-oz. arctic char or salmon fillets with skin

STEP 1 In a small skillet, toast the garlic over moderate heat, stirring occasionally, until the skins blacken, 7 to 8 minutes. Let cool slightly; discard the skins.

STEP 2 In a food processor, puree ⅓ cup of the oil with the garlic, parsley, cilantro, olives, lemon juice, cumin and paprika until smooth. Transfer the *charmoula* to a bowl and season with salt.

STEP 3 In a large nonstick skillet, heat the remaining 2 tablespoons of oil. Season the fish with salt and pepper, place it skin side down in the skillet and cook over moderately high heat until the skin is golden, about 3 minutes. Flip the fish and cook just until it flakes easily, 2 to 3 minutes longer. Drain briefly on paper towels; serve with the *charmoula*.

Prep Ahead
The *charmoula* can be refrigerated for up to 2 days.

WINE TIP
Fatty arctic char can handle pungent, herbaceous, garlicky sauces. Try this recipe with a citrusy New Zealand Sauvignon Blanc.

Curry Lobster Rolls

Cookbook author Marcia Kiesel gives the classic beach-shack lobster roll a Southeast Asian makeover by mixing curry powder, lime and fresh dill into the mayo. While crunch addicts usually tuck in potato chips, Kiesel tops her sandwich with a few crispy baked kaffir lime leaves.

TIME **45 min active; 1 hr 30 min total**	MAKES **4 servings**	CONTRIBUTED BY **Marcia Kiesel**

Two 1¼-lb. live lobsters

8 fresh or frozen kaffir lime leaves

1 Tbsp. vegetable oil, plus more for rubbing

1 large shallot, minced

3 oil-packed anchovy fillets, minced

¾ tsp. curry powder

¾ cup mayonnaise

2 tsp. fresh lime juice

1 Tbsp. chopped dill

Kosher salt

4 hot dog buns or hero rolls, split

1 Kirby cucumber, thinly sliced

STEP 1 Preheat the oven to 300°. In a large pot of boiling water, cook the lobsters until they turn bright red, about 8 minutes. Drain and let cool.

STEP 2 Twist the lobster bodies from the tails. Using scissors, cut along the underside of the shells and remove the meat. Halve the tails lengthwise and discard the dark intestines. Crack the claws and remove the meat in one piece. Remove the knuckle meat. Transfer the lobster to a bowl and refrigerate until chilled.

STEP 3 Holding a lime leaf, pull off the stem to divide the leaf in half. Repeat with the remaining leaves. Rub the leaves with oil, transfer to a baking sheet and bake until crisp, about 8 minutes.

STEP 4 In a small skillet, heat the 1 tablespoon of oil. Add the shallot and cook over moderately low heat until softened, about 2 minutes. Mash the anchovies with the shallot. Add the curry powder and cook until fragrant, about 1 minute. Scrape the mixture into a bowl and let cool. Stir in the mayonnaise, lime juice and dill and season with salt. Refrigerate for 15 minutes.

STEP 5 Fold the curry mayonnaise into the lobster. Spoon the salad into the buns, top with the lime leaves and cucumber and serve.

Thai Chicken & Wheat Berry Salad

This refreshing dish is like a Thai larb. The ground-chicken salad with wheat berries is served in fresh lettuce cups.

TIME	MAKES	CONTRIBUTED BY
20 min total	**4 servings**	**Kay Chun**

2 Tbsp. canola oil

1 lb. ground chicken, preferably dark meat

Kosher salt and pepper

½ cup cooked wheat berries or spelt

2 Tbsp. Asian fish sauce

1 Tbsp. lime juice, plus lime wedges for serving

⅓ cup chopped basil, plus whole leaves for serving

Lettuce cups, for serving

In a large nonstick skillet, heat the oil. Add the chicken, season with salt and pepper and cook over moderately high heat, stirring, until cooked through, 3 to 4 minutes. Stir in the wheat berries, fish sauce and lime juice. Remove the skillet from the heat; stir in the chopped basil. Serve the salad warm, with lettuce cups, lime wedges and basil leaves.

Chicken Roasted on Bread with Caperberries

In this super-simple sheet pan dinner, chicken legs roast on top of torn pieces of bread that absorb the rich and tangy juices, becoming deliciously crisp and chewy.

TIME	MAKES	CONTRIBUTED BY
20 min active; 1 hr 10 min total	**4 servings**	**Justin Chapple** 📷

½ lb. sourdough bread, torn into bite-size pieces

4 large shallots, quartered lengthwise

¾ cup drained caperberries

2 lemons, scrubbed and quartered lengthwise

¼ cup extra-virgin olive oil, plus more for brushing

Kosher salt and pepper

Four 12-oz. whole chicken legs

Preheat the oven to 400°. On a large rimmed baking sheet, toss the bread with the shallots, caperberries, lemons and the ¼ cup of olive oil; season with salt and pepper. Brush the chicken legs with oil and season with salt and pepper. Arrange the chicken on the bread and roast for about 50 minutes, until the bread is crisp and an instant-read thermometer inserted in the thighs registers 160°. Transfer the chicken, bread and vegetables to plates and serve.

Chicken in an Herb Garden

For this light, summery make-ahead dish, Katie Caldesi, co-author of *Rome: Centuries in an Italian Kitchen,* poaches rolled chicken breasts in vinegar before marinating them in herb-spiked olive oil. The result is silky and deeply flavorful.

TIME **30 min active; 3 hr 30 min total**	MAKES **4 servings**	CONTRIBUTED BY **Katie Caldesi**

4 skinless, boneless chicken breast halves (2 lbs.), pounded ¼ inch thick

Kosher salt and pepper

2½ cups white wine vinegar

1 cup extra-virgin olive oil

1 cup finely chopped mixed herbs, such as parsley, tarragon, basil, thyme, rosemary, sage and mint

Crusty bread, for serving

STEP 1 Season the chicken breasts with salt and pepper. Tightly roll them up lengthwise and secure with toothpicks at 1-inch intervals.

STEP 2 In a large saucepan, combine the vinegar, ³/₄ cup of water and a pinch of salt and bring to a gentle simmer. Add the chicken and cook over low heat until just white throughout, 10 to 12 minutes. Transfer the chicken to a work surface and let cool slightly. Discard the toothpicks. Slice the chicken crosswise into 1-inch-thick rounds.

STEP 3 In a large bowl, whisk the olive oil with the mixed herbs and season with salt and pepper. Add the chicken, turning to coat in the herb oil. Let cool to room temperature, about 30 minutes. Cover and refrigerate for at least 2 hours or overnight. Bring the chicken to room temperature and serve with crusty bread.

WINE TIP Many light, tart whites also have a beguiling herbal note—it can be grassy, as in Sauvignon Blanc, or more fragrant, as with Vermentino. All are good with herby dishes like this one.

CHARDONNAY
& OTHER RICH, FULL-BODIED WHITES

CHARDONNAY The most popular white wine grape in the United States, Chardonnay is in many ways a blank canvas. Around the world, its character and style vary from region to region and winemaker to winemaker, from the steely, chalky wines of Chablis to ripe and buttery California versions that fill bargain-bottle shelves. Just what Chardonnay's actual identity ought to be has been, for many years, a topic of great discussion.

Burgundy, in France, where the most sought-after Chardonnays are produced, serves as the benchmark for this variety. Here, new oak barrels tend to be used judiciously, so that they support the wine rather than overwhelm it. Unfortunately, in the 1980s and '90s, hoping to emulate Burgundy's top wines and seduced by the vanilla and spice nuances that new oak can offer, producers in other parts of the world started buying up all the barrels they could get their hands on. Industrial producers tossed in wood chips to rush the process. Many of the resulting wines were fat and clunky, tasting more like butterscotch and vanilla flavoring than fruit. Eventually, the pendulum swung back, leading to more restrained, occasionally even austere wines.

The happy medium for Chardonnay is a wine that is ripe and round, but that also has a core of refreshing acidity to keep it from flabbiness. This style of Chardonnay reveals the many virtues of the grape, one of which is that it can go fantastically well with food. There's nothing better than an herb-roasted chicken and a glass of Chardonnay, but the variety does almost as well with cheesy pastas, lobster dishes and richer fish like salmon.

VIOGNIER, MARSANNE & ROUSSANNE The best wines made from these white grapes conjure up a perfect summer day—warm sun, flowers blowing in the breeze, the peak of peach season (peach flavors are a common denominator in all three varieties). Native to France's Rhône Valley and southern France, Viognier, Marsanne and Roussanne have also seen impressive success in parts of Australia and California.

In general, all three of these white grapes produce full-bodied, lush wines. In order to find balance, producers in France will often blend them together, playing to each grape's strength. Viognier can be especially fragrant, verging on perfumey. The greatest expressions of Viognier on its own are from Condrieu, in the Rhône Valley: These are focused, texturally complex wines, not to mention quite pricey. Marsanne, which serves as the base for top whites from the northern Rhône's Hermitage region, offers beautiful nectarine and apricot flavors with a nice nutty edge. Lacking slightly for acidity, it's rarely used on its own; many winemakers blend it with the stonier, more austere Roussanne to add lift and structure.

There's nothing shy about wines made from these grapes, which means that they're at their best with substantial foods like creamy pastas, hearty chicken dishes and even some roasted meats.

CHENIN BLANC The sommelier's secret weapon, Chenin Blanc is the unsung hero of white wine, and deserves to be on more dinner tables around the world. Few grape varieties can so handily produce such varied styles of wine, from sparkling to bone-dry to off-dry to downright sweet. Originating in France's Loire Valley, Chenin has found its way to vineyards in South Africa and California, too. The best dry versions vary widely depending on where the grapes are grown, ranging from lithe and elegant to voluptuous and concentrated. But what's unwavering about Chenin is its mouthwatering fruit— think succulent pears and peaches matched with zesty, lemony acidity.

To preserve Chenin Blanc's incredible freshness, most winemakers abstain from using new oak barrels with this grape. And it's the grape's crisp intensity that makes Chenin so compelling with food. Pair it with richer fish like salmon, roast chicken, lighter pork dishes or green vegetables. Sweet versions are unparalleled in their ability to go with fruit desserts.

Smoked Trout–Caraway Rillettes

For a light and tangy smoked trout dip, skip the mayo and instead mix in labneh—yogurt that's been strained to remove all the whey, resulting in a thick, creamy spread.

TIME	MAKES	CONTRIBUTED BY
15 min total	**2½ cups**	**Kay Chun**

1½ cups labneh

2 Tbsp. minced shallot

3 Tbsp. extra-virgin olive oil

2 tsp. caraway seeds

3 thinly sliced scallions, plus more for garnish

Kosher salt and pepper

4 smoked trout fillets (12 oz.), skinned, meat flaked into large pieces

Pickled radishes and rye crackers, for serving

In a medium bowl, combine the labneh, shallot, olive oil, caraway seeds and the 3 sliced scallions; season with salt and pepper and mix well. Gently fold in the flaked trout. Garnish the rillettes with scallions and serve at room temperature with pickled radishes and rye crackers.

Make Ahead
The smoked trout rillettes can be refrigerated for 2 to 3 days. Bring to room temperature before serving.

Potatoes Stuffed with Mushrooms & Fontina

The humble baked potato gets an upgrade with melted Fontina cheese and buttery maitake, oyster and enoki mushrooms.

TIME	MAKES	CONTRIBUTED BY
10 min active; 1 hr 10 min total	**4 servings**	**Kay Chun**

4 baking potatoes, scrubbed

5 Tbsp. unsalted butter

2 Tbsp. extra-virgin olive oil

1¼ lbs. mixed tender mushrooms, such as maitake, oyster and enoki, cut into small pieces

Kosher salt and pepper

½ lb. Italian Fontina cheese, shredded (about 1 cup)

Chopped parsley, for garnish

STEP 1 Preheat the oven to 450°. On a baking sheet, bake the potatoes until tender, 1 hour.

STEP 2 Meanwhile, in a large skillet, melt 1 tablespoon of the butter in the oil. Add the mushrooms and cook over moderately high heat, stirring occasionally, until tender and golden, about 5 minutes. Season with salt and pepper.

STEP 3 Slice halfway down the length of each potato and spoon 1 tablespoon of butter and 2 tablespoons of cheese into each one. Season with salt. Top with the mushrooms and the remaining cheese. Bake for about 3 minutes, until the cheese melts. Garnish with parsley and serve hot.

Chicken & Wild Rice Soup

Even when it was 20 below and snowing, residents of Hillsboro, North Dakota, would leave their houses to get lunch at Our Town Bakery. The rotating menu included this superlative soup, for which former owner Amanda Johnson used leftover roast chicken and wild rice harvested from her husband's best friend's farm.

TIME **20 min active; 1 hr 15 min total**	MAKES **8 servings**	CONTRIBUTED BY **Amanda Johnson**

4 Tbsp. unsalted butter

3 celery ribs, cut into ½-inch pieces

2 carrots, cut into ½-inch pieces

1 medium onion, chopped

2 garlic cloves, minced

1½ tsp. finely chopped thyme

Kosher salt and pepper

¼ cup all-purpose flour

1 cup wild rice (5 oz.)

2 qts. chicken stock or low-sodium broth

4 cups bite-size pieces of roast chicken or turkey

1 cup heavy cream

STEP 1 In a large saucepan, melt the butter. Add the celery, carrots, onion, garlic, thyme and a generous pinch each of salt and pepper and cook over moderate heat, stirring occasionally, until the vegetables just start to soften, about 10 minutes. Sprinkle the flour over the vegetables and cook, stirring, until evenly coated and lightly browned, about 3 minutes.

STEP 2 Add the wild rice to the saucepan and gradually stir in the stock and 2 cups of water. Bring to a boil, then simmer over moderately low heat, stirring occasionally, until the vegetables are tender, about 30 minutes. Add the chicken and simmer, stirring occasionally, until the wild rice is tender, 10 to 15 minutes longer. Stir in the heavy cream and season with salt and pepper. Ladle the soup into bowls and serve.

Make Ahead
The chicken soup can be refrigerated for up to 2 days. Reheat gently.

WINE TIP The nutty earthiness of wild rice goes particularly well with whites that spend some time in new oak barrels, like most California Chardonnays.

Ham & Cheese Puff Pastry Tart

This crisp, rich tart is from Mimi Thorisson, the Bordeaux-based cookbook author and creator of the blog Manger. She tops store-bought puff pastry with a zippy mustard-and-shallot béchamel, then layers it with ham and cheese before baking. Think of this as a decadent croque monsieur reimagined as a savory tart.

TIME **40 min active; 1 hr 45 min total**	MAKES **4 servings**	CONTRIBUTED BY **Mimi Thorisson**

3 Tbsp. unsalted butter

1 large shallot, thinly sliced

3 Tbsp. all-purpose flour, plus more for dusting

1 cup milk

2 tsp. whole-grain mustard

Pinch of freshly grated nutmeg

Kosher salt and pepper

½ lb. all-butter puff pastry, cut in half

2 oz. Comté cheese, shredded (⅔ cup)

½ lb. thinly sliced baked ham

1 large egg yolk mixed with 1 tsp. water

STEP 1 In a medium saucepan, melt the butter. Add the sliced shallot and cook over moderate heat until softened and lightly browned, 3 to 5 minutes. Stir in the 3 tablespoons of flour and cook until bubbling, about 1 minute. Gradually whisk in the milk and bring to a boil, whisking. Cook over moderate heat, whisking frequently, until the sauce is thickened and no floury taste remains, 5 to 7 minutes. Stir in the mustard and nutmeg. Season the béchamel with salt and pepper. Let cool.

STEP 2 Line a large rimmed baking sheet with parchment paper. On a lightly floured work surface, roll out each piece of puff pastry to a 10-by-6-inch rectangle. Slide 1 pastry rectangle onto the prepared baking sheet. Spread one-third of the cooled béchamel on the first pastry, leaving a 1-inch border all around. Sprinkle half of the cheese on top and cover with half of the ham. Repeat the layering with another third of the béchamel and the remaining cheese and ham. End with a final layer of béchamel. Cover the tart with the remaining pastry and press all around the edge to seal. Crimp the edge decoratively. Using a paring knife, cut four 1-inch slits in the top of the tart, then brush all over with the egg wash. Refrigerate until chilled, about 20 minutes.

STEP 3 Preheat the oven to 450°. Bake the tart for 20 to 25 minutes, until puffed and golden brown. Let cool for 10 minutes before serving.

Prep Ahead
The recipe can be prepared through Step 2, covered loosely and refrigerated for up to 6 hours.

Pappardelle with Summer Squash & Arugula–Walnut Pesto

This recipe is a fantastic showcase for super-fresh summer squash. Simply cut zucchini and yellow squash lengthwise into ribbons on a mandoline, then toss them with hot pasta so they just barely cook.

TIME **45 min total**	MAKES **4 to 6 servings**	CONTRIBUTED BY **Kay Chun**

¾ cup walnut halves

4 cups packed arugula leaves (4 oz.)

¾ cup extra-virgin olive oil, plus more for drizzling

½ tsp. finely grated garlic

½ cup freshly grated Parmigiano-Reggiano cheese, plus shavings for garnish

Kosher salt and pepper

¾ lb. pappardelle

3 firm, fresh medium zucchini and/or yellow squash (1¼ lbs.), very thinly sliced lengthwise on a mandoline

3 Tbsp. fresh lemon juice

STEP 1 In a small skillet, toast the walnuts over moderately low heat until golden, about 5 minutes. Finely chop ½ cup of the walnuts; coarsely chop the rest for garnish.

STEP 2 In a food processor, pulse 2 cups of the arugula until finely chopped; scrape into a large bowl and stir in the ¾ cup of olive oil, the garlic, grated cheese and finely chopped walnuts. Season the pesto with salt and pepper.

STEP 3 In a large pot of salted boiling water, cook the pappardelle until al dente. Drain the pasta and add to the pesto. Add the zucchini and toss to coat. Stir in the lemon juice and the remaining 2 cups of arugula and season with salt and pepper. Transfer the pasta to a platter, drizzle with olive oil and garnish with the coarsely chopped walnuts and cheese shavings.

WINE TIP

If you love Chardonnay, consider trying white Burgundy, which is made with the same grape (many European wines are labeled by their growing region, rather than the grape variety).

Clam & Oyster Pan Roast

This aromatic seafood dish from Vivian Howard of Chef & the Farmer in Kinston, North Carolina, is a mash-up of two classics: steamed clams and New Orleans–style creamed oysters. It's hearty but not heavy, and the winter greens make it a full meal. Crusty bread is a must for sopping up the scrumptious broth.

TIME **45 min total**	MAKES **4 servings**	CONTRIBUTED BY **Vivian Howard**

4 Tbsp. unsalted butter

2 small leeks, white and tender green parts only, thinly sliced (2 cups)

Kosher salt

4 cups chopped mustard or turnip greens

4 thyme sprigs

2 garlic cloves, thinly sliced

¼ tsp. crushed red pepper

1 cup dry vermouth

2 dozen littleneck clams, scrubbed

2 dozen oysters, freshly shucked, with their liquor

2 Tbsp. heavy cream

2 Tbsp. chopped parsley

1 tsp. fresh lemon juice

2 dashes of hot sauce

Crusty bread, for serving

STEP 1 In a large enameled cast-iron casserole, melt 2 tablespoons of the butter. Add the leeks, season with salt and cook over moderate heat, stirring occasionally, until softened, about 8 minutes.

STEP 2 Add the mustard greens, thyme, garlic and crushed red pepper to the casserole and cook, stirring, until the greens are wilted, about 2 minutes.

STEP 3 Add the vermouth and clams to the casserole and bring to a boil. Cover and cook over moderate heat until the clams open, 5 to 10 minutes; transfer the clams to a bowl as they open, discarding any that do not.

STEP 4 Add the oysters and their liquor, the cream, parsley, lemon juice, hot sauce and remaining 2 tablespoons of butter to the casserole and cook just until the oysters start to curl around the edges, 1 to 2 minutes. Discard the thyme sprigs.

STEP 5 Stir the clams and any juices into the pan roast; serve immediately, with crusty bread.

End-of-Summer Eggplant Bake

Jessica Koslow of Sqirl in Los Angeles loves making this dish at the end of summer, when farmers markets are overflowing with ripe eggplant. In this modern, So-Cal take on a casserole, she bakes the eggplant until it's super tender and creamy under a topping of warm, lemony ricotta cheese and crispy croutons.

TIME **45 min total**	MAKES **4 servings**	CONTRIBUTED BY **Jessica Koslow**

2 large eggplants, cut into 1-inch cubes

½ cup plus 1 Tbsp. extra-virgin olive oil, plus more for greasing

Kosher salt and pepper

2 spring onions or 6 scallions, thinly sliced

2 Tbsp. unsalted butter, cubed

1¼ cups fresh ricotta cheese

¼ cup heavy cream

1 tsp. finely grated lemon zest plus 2 tsp. fresh lemon juice

1 Tbsp. finely chopped flat-leaf parsley

4 oz. country white bread, crusts removed and bread torn into ½-inch pieces (2 cups)

STEP 1 Preheat the oven to 450°. On 2 baking sheets, spread the eggplant in an even layer. Drizzle with 6 tablespoons of the olive oil, season with salt and pepper and toss. Roast for 10 minutes.

STEP 2 In a small bowl, toss the spring onions with 2 tablespoons of the olive oil. Add the onions to the eggplant and dot with the butter. Roast for 15 minutes longer, stirring, until the eggplant is tender.

STEP 3 In a medium bowl, stir the ricotta with the cream, lemon zest, lemon juice and parsley and season with salt and pepper. In a small bowl, toss the bread with the remaining 1 tablespoon of olive oil.

STEP 4 Lightly grease a 2-quart, 2-inch-deep baking dish. Transfer the eggplant and onions to the baking dish. Dollop with the ricotta mixture and scatter the bread on top. Bake for about 10 minutes, until the bread is golden.

Prep Ahead The roasted eggplant and onions can be refrigerated overnight. Bring to room temperature before proceeding to Step 3.

Maryland-Style Crab Cakes

These crab cakes are proportionally perfect: heavy on sweet, tender hunks of crab, light on breadcrumbs. And instead of frying the cakes, Baltimore chef Spike Gjerde of Woodberry Kitchen serves them "brold" (Baltimorese for "broiled," he says). "I can't overemphasize how important it is to use fresh, carefully processed meat from blue crabs," he adds.

TIME **35 min total**	MAKES **4 servings**	CONTRIBUTED BY **Spike Gjerde**

5 Tbsp. unsalted butter, melted

1 large egg

3 Tbsp. mayonnaise

1 tsp. fresh lemon juice, plus wedges for serving

½ tsp. salt

1 tsp. black pepper

¼ tsp. cayenne

1 lb. jumbo lump crabmeat, picked over for shells

½ cup fresh breadcrumbs

STEP 1 Preheat the broiler on the lowest setting and position a rack 12 inches from the heat. Rub 1 tablespoon of the butter on a small rimmed baking sheet.

STEP 2 In a large bowl, whisk the egg with the mayonnaise, lemon juice, salt, black pepper and cayenne. Gently fold in the crabmeat and ¼ cup of the breadcrumbs, breaking up the crab into smaller pieces. Refrigerate for 10 minutes.

STEP 3 Pack one-fourth of the crab mixture into a ½-cup dry measuring cup and turn out onto the prepared baking sheet. With slightly damp hands, gently form it into a patty. Repeat with the remaining crab mixture; the patties will be very loose. Sprinkle the remaining ¼ cup of breadcrumbs on top of the patties.

STEP 4 Broil the crab cakes for 5 minutes, until the crumbs are golden. Drizzle the remaining 4 tablespoons of butter on top and broil for 1 minute longer. With a large spatula, carefully transfer the crab cakes to plates. Serve with lemon wedges.

Grilled Lobsters with Miso–Chile Butter

When cooking for a crowd, *Top Chef* judge Gail Simmons has her fishmonger clean and halve the lobsters before grilling. "It really cuts down on the work and mess," she says.

TIME **40 min total**	MAKES **4 servings**	CONTRIBUTED BY **Gail Simmons**

1 stick unsalted butter, cubed

2 Tbsp. shiro (white) miso

1 Tbsp. Sriracha

2 Tbsp. fresh lemon juice, plus wedges for serving

2 bunches of scallions

1 Tbsp. canola oil

Kosher salt and pepper

8 long metal skewers

Four 1½-lb. lobsters, halved lengthwise, claws detached and reserved

STEP 1 In a small saucepan, melt the butter. Whisk in the miso, Sriracha and lemon juice. Reserve ¼ cup of the miso-chile butter for serving.

STEP 2 Light a grill. In a large bowl, toss the scallions with the oil and season with salt and pepper. Grill over moderate heat, turning, until lightly charred and tender, about 5 minutes. Chop the scallions and toss with 1 tablespoon of the miso-chile butter.

STEP 3 Skewer the lobster bodies from the tail to the head to keep them straight. Brush the lobster meat with 2 tablespoons of the miso-chile butter. Grill the lobster bodies and claws over moderate heat, turning and basting the meat with the remaining miso-chile butter, until the shells are bright red, 7 to 8 minutes for the tails and 12 to 15 minutes for the claws. Remove the skewers.

STEP 4 Arrange the lobsters on a platter or plates and scatter the scallions on top. Serve with lemon wedges and the reserved ¼ cup of miso-chile butter.

WINE TIP Rich, buttery sauces (or just melted butter) ask for a wine with equal richness, like a ripe New World Chardonnay.

Swordfish Skewers with Salsa Verde

For these skewers, L.A. chef Chad Colby tucks fresh bay leaves between cubes of swordfish and ribbons of zucchini—the herbs impart a lovely fragrance to the dish. You can buy fresh bay leaves at some specialty food shops, Indian or Mediterranean markets and online from amazon.com.

TIME	MAKES	CONTRIBUTED BY
45 min active; 1 hr 45 min total	**4 servings**	**Chad Colby**

1 cup flat-leaf parsley leaves

10 garlic cloves, crushed

1 tsp. crushed red pepper

½ cup extra-virgin olive oil

Kosher salt and black pepper

4 long metal skewers

28 fresh bay leaves (1 cup)

1½ lbs. swordfish, cut into 1½-inch pieces

1 medium zucchini, very thinly sliced lengthwise on a mandoline

2 lemons, halved crosswise

STEP 1 In a blender or mini food processor, pulse the parsley, garlic, crushed red pepper and olive oil to a thick puree. Season with salt and black pepper and transfer the sauce to a bowl.

STEP 2 Onto each of the skewers, alternately thread a bay leaf, a piece of swordfish, another bay leaf and a slice of zucchini, repeating until each skewer has 3 pieces of fish, 3 slices of zucchini and 7 bay leaves. Season the skewers with salt and black pepper and brush all over with the parsley sauce. Cover and refrigerate for 1 hour.

STEP 3 Light a grill or heat a grill pan. Grill the skewers over moderate heat, turning, until the fish is lightly browned and cooked through, about 6 minutes. Transfer the skewers to a platter. Meanwhile, grill the lemon halves cut side down until charred, about 2 minutes. Serve the skewers with the grilled lemons. Discard the bay leaves.

WINE TIP

To pair with this Mediterranean-inspired dish, try a white from the warm regions of southern France, like a Côtes du Rhône blanc.

Steamed Bass with Spicy Butter

Topping sea bass with pats of spiced butter before steaming results in an instant sauce as they melt into the fragrant fish and mingle with the lime juice.

TIME	MAKES	CONTRIBUTED BY
30 min total	**4 servings**	**Grace Parisi**

Four 7-oz. sea bass or red snapper fillets with skin

One 1½-inch piece of fresh ginger, peeled and cut into very thin matchsticks

1 serrano chile, thinly sliced

1 small garlic clove, minced

Finely grated zest and juice of 1 lime

Kosher salt and pepper

4 Tbsp. unsalted butter, cut into small pieces

Chopped cilantro leaves and sliced scallion, for garnish

STEP 1 With a knife, make 4 shallow slashes in the skin of each fish fillet and place them in a large glass or ceramic pie plate, skin side up. In a small bowl, combine the ginger, chile, garlic and lime zest and sprinkle the mixture over the fish. Season with salt and pepper and dot with the butter. Drizzle the lime juice on top.

STEP 2 Make a steamer by arranging 3 small balls of aluminum foil in a very large, deep skillet. Add 1 inch of water to the skillet and bring to a boil. Carefully set the pie plate on the foil balls, cover the skillet with a tight-fitting lid or aluminum foil and steam for about 5 minutes, until the fish flakes with a fork. Using a spatula, transfer the fillets to shallow bowls and spoon the buttery broth on top. Garnish with cilantro and scallion and serve.

Easy Persian Fried Fish

In this super-simple recipe adapted from Naomi Duguid's *Taste of Persia*, turmeric tints the fish a vibrant yellow, but it's the aromatic fenugreek leaves that give it a distinctive flavor.

TIME	MAKES	CONTRIBUTED BY
20 min total	**4 servings**	**Naomi Duguid**

¼ cup all-purpose flour

1 Tbsp. crumbled fenugreek leaves

½ Tbsp. dried mint

½ Tbsp. dried dill

½ Tbsp. dried thyme

½ tsp. cayenne

¼ tsp. ground turmeric

Four 6-oz. red snapper (or other white fish) fillets with skin

Kosher salt and pepper

¼ cup vegetable oil

Lemon wedges and greens, for serving

STEP 1 In a shallow bowl, whisk the flour with the fenugreek, mint, dill, thyme, cayenne and turmeric. Season the fish with salt and pepper; dredge in the flour.

STEP 2 In a large cast-iron skillet, heat the oil until shimmering. Add the fish skin side down and press with a spatula to flatten. Cook over moderately high heat until the skin is browned, about 4 minutes. Turn the fish and cook until white throughout, about 2 minutes longer. Serve with lemon wedges and greens.

Turkey Tonnato

In this easy riff on the classic chilled Italian dish vitello tonnato, roast turkey replaces veal, and chickpeas and yogurt give the canned-tuna sauce extra oomph.

TIME	MAKES	CONTRIBUTED BY
20 min total	**4 servings**	**Kay Chun**

1 lb. thinly sliced roast turkey breast

One 6½-oz. can tuna in water, drained

½ cup canned chickpeas, rinsed

¼ cup plain yogurt

½ cup extra-virgin olive oil

¼ cup chopped drained capers

½ cup chopped mixed herbs, such as tarragon, chives and dill

Kosher salt and pepper

Arrange the turkey slices on a platter. In a food processor, combine the tuna, chickpeas and yogurt. With the machine on, drizzle in the oil until smooth. Transfer the sauce to a bowl, stir in the capers and herbs and season with salt and pepper. Spoon over the turkey and serve.

Ham Glazed with Cider & Cloves

"As a gift to my family at Christmas, I cook everyone's favorite dish and teach them how to make it," says TV chef Carla Hall. For her husband, it's this spiral-cut ham glazed with cider, brown sugar, mustard, bourbon and spices.

TIME	MAKES	CONTRIBUTED BY
30 min active; 2 hr total	**12 servings**	**Carla Hall**

One 7- to 8-lb. spiral-cut ham

1 cup fresh apple cider

½ cup light brown sugar

3 Tbsp. unsalted butter

2 Tbsp. Dijon mustard

2 Tbsp. bourbon

1 Tbsp. apple cider vinegar

One 3-inch cinnamon stick

6 whole cloves

½ tsp. black peppercorns

½ tsp. freshly grated nutmeg

STEP 1 Preheat the oven to 375°. Place the ham in a 9-by-13-inch baking dish. In a small saucepan, combine all of the remaining ingredients and bring to a simmer, whisking occasionally. Cook over moderately low heat until reduced to ¾ cup, about 25 minutes. Pour the glaze over the ham, leaving the spices on the meat. Cover tightly with foil. Bake for about 1 hour and 15 minutes, basting every 15 minutes, until heated through. Transfer the ham to a platter.

STEP 2 Strain the pan juices into a small saucepan. Bring to a boil and cook until reduced to a glaze, 8 to 10 minutes. Spoon the glaze over the ham and serve.

Prep Ahead
The first glaze can be made 2 days ahead and stored in the refrigerator. Rewarm before using.

Pan-Roasted Chicken with Tarragon Crème Fraîche

WINE TIP

Generally, warmer climates result in bigger, richer wines. Look, for instance, to California's Central Coast for a white to pair here.

Cookbook author Jane Sigal created this recipe based on a dish she fell in love with at the Paris wine bar Coinstot Vino. The key is the aromatic spice mixture that seasons the chicken breasts before they're sautéed. Don't reduce the crème fraîche that finishes the dish; just make sure it's heated through before serving.

TIME	MAKES	CONTRIBUTED BY
30 min active; 1 hr 20 min total	**4 servings**	**Jane Sigal**

1 tsp. coriander seeds

1 tsp. yellow mustard seeds

1 tsp. black peppercorns

1 tsp. dried summer savory or dried oregano

4 medium fingerling potatoes, halved lengthwise

2 medium carrots, sliced diagonally 1 inch thick

¼ head of cauliflower, cut into 1½-inch florets

¼ lb. haricots verts or thin green beans

5 Tbsp. unsalted butter

1 Tbsp. fresh lemon juice

Kosher salt and pepper

4 boneless chicken breast halves with skin

¼ cup chicken stock or low-sodium broth

½ cup crème fraîche

¼ cup chopped tarragon

STEP 1 In a spice grinder, combine the coriander and mustard seeds with the peppercorns and summer savory and grind to a powder.

STEP 2 Set a steamer basket in a wide pot and bring 1 inch of water to a simmer. Layer the vegetables in the basket starting with the potatoes, then the carrots, cauliflower and beans. Cover and steam over moderate heat until the beans are just tender, about 3 minutes; transfer the beans to a bowl. Steam until the cauliflower is tender, about 3 minutes more; add to the bowl. Steam the carrots and potatoes until tender, 10 minutes longer; add to the bowl.

STEP 3 In a large skillet, melt 2 tablespoons of the butter. Add the steamed vegetables and cook over moderately high heat, tossing, until heated through and coated with butter, about 1 minute. Add the lemon juice and season with salt and pepper.

STEP 4 Season the chicken breasts with salt and pepper and coat all over with the ground spices. In another large skillet, melt the remaining 3 tablespoons of butter. Add the chicken breasts skin side down and cook over moderately

low heat until the skin is well browned, about 12 minutes. Turn the chicken and cook, basting a few times, until just cooked through, about 7 minutes longer. Transfer the chicken to a platter.

STEP 5 Rewarm the vegetables. Add the stock to the skillet used to cook the chicken and boil over high heat for 2 minutes, scraping up any browned bits. Add the crème fraîche and bring to a boil, stirring. Remove the skillet from the heat and stir in the tarragon. Season with salt and pepper. Spoon the sauce over the chicken, mound the vegetables alongside and serve.

Prep Ahead

The recipe can be prepared 1 day ahead through Step 2. Keep the spice mixture at room temperature; refrigerate the steamed vegetables.

Roast Chicken with Salsa Verde & Roasted Lemons

"There will be a chicken on my headstone, I'm so well-known for it," says chef Jonathan Waxman of Barbuto in New York City. This crisp and juicy bird with a chunky seven-herb salsa verde is a favorite variation on the roast chicken that put him on the culinary map.

TIME **40 min active; 1 hr total**	MAKES **4 servings**	CONTRIBUTED BY **Jonathan Waxman**

One 4-lb. chicken, backbone removed, chicken halved lengthwise

1 cup plus 2 Tbsp. extra-virgin olive oil

Kosher salt and pepper

2 lemons, halved crosswise

¼ cup capers, rinsed

4 anchovy fillets in oil, drained

3 garlic cloves, crushed

½ cup coarsely chopped arugula

½ cup coarsely chopped parsley

½ cup coarsely chopped basil

½ cup coarsely chopped cilantro

¼ cup coarsely chopped tarragon

¼ cup coarsely chopped chives

¼ cup coarsely chopped sage

STEP 1 Preheat the oven to 450°. Arrange the chicken skin side up on a rack set over a baking sheet. Rub with 2 tablespoons of the olive oil; season with salt and pepper. Place the lemons cut side down on the rack. Roast the chicken for about 40 minutes, until golden and cooked through. Let rest for 10 minutes.

STEP 2 Meanwhile, in a mortar or blender, mash the capers with the anchovies and garlic until a paste forms. Transfer to a medium bowl and whisk in the remaining 1 cup of olive oil. Stir in the herbs; season with salt.

STEP 3 Carve the chicken; arrange on a platter with the lemons. Serve with the salsa verde.

Prep Ahead

The salsa verde can be refrigerated overnight; serve at room temperature.

LIGHTLY SWEET WINES

RIESLING Even though dry versions of Riesling are most popular these days, open your mind to trying one with just a touch of sweetness. Let's be honest: Humans like sugar. That's why a fruity, lightly sweet (or "off-dry") yet still vibrant Riesling will have you ready to plunge a straw right into the bottle. The little hit of sweetness in these wines marries beautifully with dishes that are salty or have some heat, which means they're a great match for anything fried (chicken, oysters, potatoes) or spicy (Thai curries, hot wings). They'll even go with dishes that have a little sweetness of their own, like barbecue. For the longest time, it was difficult to know where a Riesling fell on the sweetness scale by simply looking at the bottle, but many regions, including most of Germany, Austria, Washington state and New Zealand, have come around to putting this info on the back label.

GEWÜRZTRAMINER Gewürztraminer often gets a bad rap for being too flamboyantly perfumed. While it's true that in the wrong hands the grape can produce wines that smell like rose-scented face cream, a great winemaker's Gewürztraminer can offer a transporting combination of grapefruit-like acidity, juicy pear fruit and just a hint of flowers and gingery spice. The grape has its roots in France's Alsace region, where the local specialty is tarte flambée, a flatbread topped with caramelized onions, crisp bacon and Gruyère cheese—exactly the sort of food a slightly sweet Gewürztraminer calls for. American versions of Gewürztraminer tend to be a little more restrained than their very full-bodied French counterparts, with orange citrus and baking-spice flavors at the forefront.

Coconut Rice Bowl with Chicken

This quick, all-in-one meal combines fragrant coconut rice with shredded chicken and crunchy cucumbers.

TIME	MAKES	CONTRIBUTED BY
10 min active; 40 min total	**4 servings**	**Kay Chun**

1 cup jasmine rice

2 cups unsweetened coconut milk

1 Tbsp. sugar

Kosher salt

2 cups shredded cooked chicken

2 small Kirby cucumbers, chopped

1 Tbsp. canola oil

Chopped scallions, for garnish

In a large saucepan, combine the rice, coconut milk, sugar and ½ teaspoon of salt and bring to a boil. Cover and cook over low heat until the rice is tender and all of the coconut milk is absorbed, about 20 minutes. Remove from the heat and let the rice stand for 10 minutes. Transfer to a bowl and stir in the chicken, cucumbers and oil. Season with salt, garnish with scallions and serve.

Sweet & Sticky Hot Wings

We love these finger-licking-good wings—they're layered with spice throughout: smoked paprika in the coating, hot sauce and pepper jelly in the delightfully sticky glaze.

TIME	MAKES	CONTRIBUTED BY
15 min active; 1 hr total	**2 to 4 servings**	**Grace Parisi**

Nonstick cooking spray

2 Tbsp. all-purpose flour

1 tsp. salt

1 tsp. smoked paprika

½ tsp. dried garlic

½ tsp. dried onion

2 lbs. chicken wingettes and drumettes (see Note)

2½ Tbsp. red hot sauce, preferably Frank's RedHot

2 Tbsp. unsalted butter, melted

2 Tbsp. hot pepper jelly, melted

STEP 1 Preheat the oven to 500°. Line a large baking sheet with foil and coat with nonstick spray. In a large bowl, mix the flour with the salt, paprika, garlic and onion. Add the chicken and toss to coat. Spread the chicken on the prepared baking sheet and lightly coat with nonstick spray. Roast the chicken for 45 minutes, turning once or twice, until browned and crispy.

STEP 2 In a large bowl, whisk the hot sauce with the butter and hot pepper jelly. Add the chicken wings, toss and serve.

Note
Wingettes and drumettes are often sold separately.

Bacon & Egg Pizza

South Carolina chef Jesse Sutton scrambles his eggs the French way—slowly, with lots of butter. He spoons the custardy eggs onto a pizza topped with crème fraîche, Brie, mozzarella and bacon. This outrageous pie is exactly what you want to serve if you're in the mood for a wine-soaked brunch.

WINE TIP The best wine for this over-the-top dish has a touch of sugar to match the food's richness.

TIME **45 min total**	MAKES **One 12-inch pizza**	CONTRIBUTED BY **Jesse Sutton**

6 oz. thick-sliced bacon, cut crosswise into ⅓-inch lardons

4 large eggs

1 Tbsp. heavy cream

Kosher salt

2 Tbsp. unsalted butter

All-purpose flour, for dusting

1 lb. pizza dough

⅓ cup crème fraîche

3 oz. Brie, thinly sliced (with rind, if desired)

2 oz. fresh mozzarella, shredded

Snipped chives, for garnish

STEP 1 Set a pizza stone in the oven and preheat the oven to 500°. Spread the bacon in a pie plate and bake for 15 minutes, stirring once, until nearly crisp. Drain on paper towels.

STEP 2 Meanwhile, in a bowl, whisk the eggs with the cream and a pinch of salt. In a medium nonstick skillet, cook the eggs and 1 tablespoon of the butter over low heat, whisking frequently, until small curds form and the eggs are creamy, about 12 minutes. Remove the eggs from the heat. Stir in the remaining 1 tablespoon of butter and season with salt.

STEP 3 On a lightly floured work surface, stretch out the pizza dough to a 12-inch round and transfer to a lightly floured pizza peel. Spread the crème fraîche evenly over the dough, leaving a 1-inch border all around. Top with the crispy bacon, Brie and mozzarella.

STEP 4 Slide the pizza onto the hot stone and bake for about 7 minutes, until lightly golden and bubbling. Remove the pizza from the oven and spoon the scrambled eggs on top. Slide the pizza back onto the stone and bake for about 2 minutes longer, until the eggs are hot. Garnish with chives, cut into wedges and serve.

Moo Shu Shrimp

Making cookbook author Grace Parisi's rendition of the Chinese restaurant standby is even faster than waiting for delivery—thanks to the brilliant use of packaged coleslaw mix and presliced mushrooms. You can find moo shu pancakes in the frozen section of Asian markets, but small flour tortillas are a perfect cross-cultural substitute.

TIME	MAKES	CONTRIBUTED BY
40 min total	**4 servings**	**Grace Parisi**

12 small flour tortillas

¼ cup plus 2 Tbsp. vegetable oil

1 lb. shelled and deveined medium shrimp

3 large eggs, beaten

Kosher salt and pepper

2 Tbsp. minced peeled fresh ginger

1 large garlic clove, minced

3 oz. sliced mixed wild mushrooms (1 packed cup)

8 oz. shredded coleslaw mix (3 cups)

3 scallions, halved lengthwise and cut into 1-inch lengths

1 Tbsp. hoisin sauce, plus more for serving

Cilantro leaves, for serving

STEP 1 Preheat the oven to 200°. Stack and wrap the tortillas in foil and heat until warmed through.

STEP 2 Heat a large wok or skillet until very hot to the touch. Add 1 tablespoon of the oil and heat until smoking. Add the shrimp and stir-fry over high heat until lightly browned and cooked through, about 2 minutes. Scrape the shrimp onto a large platter. Add 2 tablespoons of the oil to the wok. Stir the eggs, season them with salt and pepper and add to the wok. Cook the eggs, stirring, until large soft curds form, about 2 minutes. Scrape the eggs onto the platter with the shrimp.

STEP 3 Add 2 tablespoons of the oil to the wok. Add the ginger, garlic and mushrooms and stir-fry over high heat until lightly browned, about 4 minutes. Add the remaining 1 tablespoon of oil. Add the coleslaw mix and scallions, season with salt and pepper and stir-fry until the cabbage is just wilted but still crunchy, about 4 minutes. Return the shrimp and eggs to the wok, add the 1 tablespoon of hoisin sauce and stir-fry just until combined. Transfer the moo shu shrimp to a large bowl and serve with the warmed tortillas, cilantro leaves and hoisin sauce.

Spring Rolls with Pork & Glass Noodles

Danny Bowien of Mission Chinese Food in San Francisco and NYC got the inspiration for this recipe by watching one of Oklahoma City's best Vietnamese cooks make spring rolls at home. They're stuffed with ground pork, glass noodles and a secret ingredient: sweet, crunchy taro.

TIME **1 hr total**	MAKES **12 rolls**	CONTRIBUTED BY **Danny Bowien**

2 oz. glass (cellophane) noodles

¾ lb. ground pork

½ cup julienned carrots (about 1 small)

½ cup finely shredded green cabbage

½ cup thinly sliced yellow onion (½ small)

½ cup julienned taro or potato

2 Tbsp. oyster sauce

1½ tsp. kosher salt

1 tsp. sugar

½ tsp. freshly ground pepper

Vegetable oil, for frying

Twelve 7-inch square spring roll wrappers

1 large egg, lightly beaten

Chinese hot mustard and/or sweet chile sauce, for dipping

STEP 1 In a small saucepan of boiling water, cook the noodles until al dente, 4 to 5 minutes. Drain and transfer to a bowl of ice water to cool. Drain the noodles well and chop into 3-inch pieces.

STEP 2 Transfer the noodles to a large bowl and add all of the remaining ingredients except the vegetable oil, spring roll wrappers, beaten egg and dipping condiments; mix well.

STEP 3 In a large enameled cast-iron casserole, heat 2 inches of oil to 350°. Place 1 wrapper on a work surface with a corner facing you; keep the remaining wrappers covered with a damp clean kitchen towel. Spoon ¼ cup of the filling in the lower third of the wrapper. Bring the corner up and over the filling and roll up, folding in the sides as you roll. Dab the top corner with the beaten egg and press to seal the spring roll. Repeat with the remaining wrappers and filling.

STEP 4 Fry the spring rolls in the hot oil, turning occasionally, until golden and crispy and the pork is cooked through, about 5 minutes. Drain the spring rolls on a paper towel–lined baking sheet and serve with hot mustard and/or sweet chile sauce.

Prep Ahead

The uncooked spring rolls can be refrigerated for up to 4 hours; keep covered with a damp cloth.

Drunken Noodles

A popular street food in Thailand, *pad kee mao* contains no alcohol. This recipe from Bank Atcharawan of The Patio Desserts & Drinks in Las Vegas is made with broad rice noodles, tofu, chiles and Thai basil, and supports the theory that the super-fiery noodles got their name because they are great to snack on with drinks.

TIME	MAKES	CONTRIBUTED BY
45 min total	**4 servings**	**Bank Atcharawan**

Vegetable oil, for stir-frying

7 oz. firm tofu, cubed and dried

½ cup chicken stock or low-sodium broth

1 Tbsp. oyster sauce

1 Tbsp. Asian fish sauce

1½ tsp. roasted red chile paste (see Note)

1 tsp. black soy sauce (see Note) or ¾ tsp. soy sauce sweetened with ¼ tsp. molasses

½ tsp. sugar

½ red bell pepper, seeded and sliced

½ large jalapeño, seeded and sliced

2 garlic cloves, minced

1 red Thai bird chile, minced

½ lb. pad thai rice noodles, cooked and cut in half crosswise

1 cup Thai basil leaves, plus more for garnish

Lime wedges, for serving

STEP 1 In a nonstick skillet, heat ¼ inch of oil. Add the tofu and cook over moderately high heat, turning, until crisp, about 5 minutes. Drain on paper towels.

STEP 2 In a small bowl, whisk the stock, oyster sauce, fish sauce, chile paste, soy sauce and sugar.

STEP 3 In a large skillet, heat 2 tablespoons of oil. Add the bell pepper, jalapeño, garlic and Thai chile and stir-fry over high heat until fragrant, about 2 minutes. Add the noodles and stir-fry until browned, about 4 minutes. Add the sauce and toss over moderately high heat until absorbed. Fold in the 1 cup of basil and the tofu. Garnish with more basil and serve with lime wedges.

Note
Roasted red chile paste and black soy sauce are available at most Asian markets and online from kalustyans.com.

WINE TIP
Spicy Asian dishes pair best with a white that has a little sweetness to counter the burn. In this case, try a German Kabinett Riesling.

Vermicelli with Chicken Skewers & Nuoc Cham

Vietnamese *banh hoi* (cool rice vermicelli served with meat) is the ultimate customizable meal. Piles of cucumber, fresh herbs and grilled chicken are arranged on a platter of vermicelli and bean sprouts and drizzled with tangy nuoc cham sauce. As each diner takes a portion, the components mingle and become even more delicious.

TIME	MAKES	CONTRIBUTED BY
40 min total	**4 servings**	**F&W Test Kitchen**

5 Tbsp. Asian fish sauce
(nuoc mam or nam pla; see Note)

2 Tbsp. sugar

3 garlic cloves, minced

1 Tbsp. vegetable oil

1 lb. skinless, boneless chicken breast halves, cut lengthwise into 12 strips

12 long wooden skewers, soaked in water for 1 hour

½ tsp. crushed red pepper

1 tsp. wine vinegar

2 Tbsp. plus 1 tsp. fresh lime juice (from about 2 limes)

½ lb. vermicelli

1 cup bean sprouts

1 cucumber—peeled, halved lengthwise, seeded and thinly sliced

⅔ cup mint, basil or cilantro leaves, or any combination of these

⅓ cup chopped peanuts

STEP 1 Heat the broiler or light the grill. In a medium bowl, combine 1 tablespoon of the fish sauce, 1 tablespoon of the sugar, 2 of the garlic cloves and the oil. Add the chicken and toss, then thread each strip onto a skewer. Broil or grill the chicken until just done, about 2 minutes per side.

STEP 2 In a small bowl, combine the remaining 4 tablespoons of fish sauce, 1 tablespoon of sugar and 1 garlic clove with the crushed red pepper, vinegar, lime juice and 2 tablespoons of water. Set the nuoc cham aside.

STEP 3 In a pot of salted boiling water, cook the vermicelli until just done, about 9 minutes. Add the bean sprouts during the last minute of cooking. Drain the vermicelli and bean sprouts, rinse with cold water and drain thoroughly.

STEP 4 Arrange the vermicelli and bean sprouts on a platter and top with the cucumber, herbs and chicken skewers. Pour the nuoc cham on top, sprinkle with the peanuts and serve.

Note
Asian fish sauce is available at Asian markets and many large supermarkets.

Honey–Ginger Chicken with Lime

This easy weeknight chicken dish from New Delhi–born chef Suvir Saran is tangy and sweet, with aromatic hints of ginger and lime. Be sure to serve it with rice or naan—you'll want to soak up every last bit.

TIME **45 min total**	MAKES **4 servings**	CONTRIBUTED BY **Suvir Saran**	

2 Tbsp. balsamic vinegar

1 Tbsp. honey

⅓ cup minced peeled fresh ginger

1 jalapeño, finely chopped

2 tsp. garam masala

1½ tsp. ground coriander

1 tsp. ground cumin

½ tsp. cayenne

1 Tbsp. plus 1 tsp. salt

1 tsp. cracked black pepper

3½ tsp. finely grated lime zest

4 chicken legs, cut into drumsticks and thighs

2 tsp. sugar

4 Tbsp. unsalted butter

2 Tbsp. canola oil

2 Tbsp. fresh lime juice

Lime wedges, for serving

STEP 1 Preheat the oven to 400°. In a large bowl, whisk the vinegar, honey, ginger, jalapeño, garam masala, coriander, cumin, cayenne, salt, black pepper and 3 teaspoons of the lime zest. Prick the chicken with a fork, add it to the bowl and toss. In a small bowl, mix the sugar with the remaining ½ teaspoon of lime zest.

STEP 2 In a large ovenproof skillet, melt 2 tablespoons of the butter in the oil over moderately high heat. Add the chicken and cook, turning, until golden, about 5 minutes. Sprinkle with the lime sugar, transfer to the oven and roast for 25 minutes, until the chicken is cooked through.

STEP 3 Stir the lime juice and the remaining 2 tablespoons of butter into the skillet. Serve the chicken with the pan juices and lime wedges.

WINE **TIP** The fragrant spice aromas of a lightly sweet Gewürztraminer often play beautifully against Indian seasonings like the garam masala here.

Coq au Riesling

In his creamy, white wine take on coq au vin, Portland, Oregon, chef Christopher Israel braises chicken legs in dry Riesling. For an extra-luscious sauce, he whisks silky-rich crème fraîche into the cooking juices.

TIME	MAKES	CONTRIBUTED BY
45 min active; 1 hr 30 min total	**4 to 6 servings**	**Christopher Israel**

4 lbs. chicken legs, split

Kosher salt and pepper

¼ cup canola oil

1 medium onion, chopped

1 medium carrot, chopped

1 celery rib, chopped

2 medium shallots, chopped

1½ cups dry Riesling

1½ cups chicken stock or low-sodium broth

4 thyme sprigs

2 Tbsp. unsalted butter

2 Tbsp. extra-virgin olive oil

1 lb. mixed mushrooms, sliced

½ cup crème fraîche

2 tsp. fresh lemon juice

Finely chopped tarragon, for garnish

STEP 1 Preheat the oven to 300°. Season the chicken with salt and pepper. In a large enameled cast-iron casserole, heat 2 tablespoons of the canola oil. Add half of the chicken and cook over moderately high heat, turning, until browned, about 8 minutes. Transfer to a plate. Cook the remaining chicken, then pour off the fat and wipe out the casserole.

STEP 2 Heat the remaining 2 tablespoons of canola oil in the casserole. Add the onion, carrot, celery and shallots and cook over moderate heat, stirring, until the vegetables are softened and lightly browned, about 8 minutes. Add the wine and simmer for 1 minute, scraping up the browned bits from the pot. Add the stock and thyme and bring to a boil.

STEP 3 Nestle the chicken in the casserole, cover and braise in the oven for 1 hour, until tender.

STEP 4 Meanwhile, in a very large skillet, melt the butter in the olive oil. Add the mushrooms and cook over high heat, without stirring, until well browned, about 5 minutes. Season the mushrooms with salt and pepper and cook, stirring, until tender, 3 to 5 minutes; transfer to a plate.

STEP 5 Transfer the chicken to a plate. Strain the braising liquid through a fine sieve into a heatproof bowl, pressing on the solids; skim off the fat. Return the braising liquid to the casserole and boil until reduced to 1½ cups, 3 to 5 minutes. Whisk in the crème fraîche and lemon juice and season with salt and pepper. Add the mushrooms and chicken to the sauce and simmer for about 3 minutes. Garnish with chopped tarragon and serve.

Turkey Curry Soup

This quick stew, fragrant with curry, lime and herbs, makes excellent use of leftover roast turkey.

TIME **30 min total**	MAKES **4 servings**	CONTRIBUTED BY **Kay Chun** 📷

2 Tbsp. canola oil

2 Tbsp. Thai red curry paste

½ small kabocha squash (1 lb.)—peeled, seeded and cut into 1½-inch pieces (4 cups)

1 cup unsweetened coconut milk

1 Tbsp. Asian fish sauce

3 cups (¾ lb.) shredded roasted turkey

3 Tbsp. fresh lime juice

½ cup chopped mixed herbs, such as cilantro and basil

Kosher salt and pepper

In a large saucepan, heat the oil. Add the curry paste and squash and cook over high heat, stirring, until lightly caramelized, about 3 minutes. Add the coconut milk, fish sauce and 4 cups of water and bring to a boil. Cover and simmer until the squash is tender, about 15 minutes. Stir in the turkey, lime juice and herbs, season with salt and pepper and serve.

Sichuan-Style Green Beans with Pork

Three key ingredients make up this spicy stir-fry from F&W's Justin Chapple: ground pork, green beans and dried hot red chiles. To round it out, Chapple adds garlic, soy sauce and lime juice. The stir-fry is perfect with freshly steamed white or brown rice or over rice noodles.

TIME **30 min total**	MAKES **4 servings**	CONTRIBUTED BY **Justin Chapple**

2 Tbsp. canola oil

½ lb. ground pork

¾ lb. green beans, thinly sliced crosswise

7 to 10 dried Chinese hot red chiles, cracked

2 garlic cloves, minced

1½ Tbsp. soy sauce

1½ Tbsp. fresh lime juice

Kosher salt and white pepper

Steamed rice, for serving

In a large skillet, heat the oil until shimmering. Add the ground pork and cook over moderately high heat, breaking it up with a fork, until nearly cooked through, about 5 minutes. Add the green beans, red chiles and garlic and stir-fry over high heat until the green beans are crisp-tender, about 7 minutes. Stir in the soy sauce and lime juice and season with salt and white pepper. Serve with steamed rice.

Ham & Gruyère French Toast Sandwiches

WINE
TIP

Surprisingly, dishes with sweetness are often best with lightly sweet wines–they make dry wines taste harsh and acidic.

Dive into this over-the-top sandwich with a fork and knife or pick it up with your hands, providing you've got plenty of napkins at the ready. Chef Jesse Ziff Cool of Flea St. Café in Menlo Park, California, likes to tuck the maple-simmered apples in with the ham and cheese, but the fruit can be served on the side, along with a spicy mustard.

TIME **40 min total**	MAKES **4 servings**	CONTRIBUTED BY **Jesse Ziff Cool**

2 Granny Smith apples—peeled, cored and thinly sliced

¼ cup pure maple syrup

One 3-inch cinnamon stick

⅔ cup milk

2 large eggs, beaten

Eight ½-inch-thick hand-cut slices from a loaf of white bread

Dijon mustard, for spreading

6 oz. sliced Gruyère cheese

½ lb. thickly sliced smoked ham

1 to 2 Tbsp. unsalted butter

STEP 1 In a medium saucepan, combine the apples, maple syrup, cinnamon stick and 1 cup of water and bring to a boil. Simmer over moderately low heat, stirring occasionally, until the apples are tender, about 6 minutes. Using a slotted spoon, transfer the apples to a bowl and let cool to room temperature.

STEP 2 In a shallow bowl, whisk the milk and eggs. Spread 4 slices of the bread with mustard. Top with half of the cheese, the ham and then the remaining cheese.

STEP 3 In a large skillet, melt 1 tablespoon of the butter over low heat. Dip the bottoms of the 4 topped bread slices in the beaten egg until just saturated and transfer to the skillet. Dip the remaining slices of bread on 1 side only and place them, soaked side up, on the sandwiches. Cover the skillet and cook over moderately low heat until the bread is browned on the bottom, about 3 minutes. Turn the sandwiches, adding more

butter to the skillet if necessary. Cover and cook until the second side is browned and the cheese is melted, about 3 minutes longer. Transfer the sandwiches to a cutting board and let stand for 5 minutes. Cut in half and serve with the maple apples.

Prep Ahead
The apples can be refrigerated in the poaching liquid for up to 1 day; drain just before using.

Serve With
Steamed or sautéed greens.

Sausage Choucroute

Choucroute is a classic Alsatian comfort food made with sauerkraut, boiled potatoes and half a dozen types of sausage and smoked meat. It can take hours to cook, but this shortcut version is ready in less than 60 minutes.

TIME	MAKES	CONTRIBUTED BY
10 min active; 55 min total	**4 servings**	**Kay Chun**

1 lb. mixed sausages, such as bratwurst and fresh chorizo

1 lb. small Yukon Gold potatoes, quartered

One 25-oz. jar of sauerkraut, drained (3 cups)

2 Tbsp. extra-virgin olive oil

1 tsp. caraway seeds

Kosher salt and pepper

Crusty bread and grainy mustard, for serving

Preheat the oven to 425°. In a large cast-iron skillet, toss the sausages with the potatoes, sauerkraut, olive oil and caraway seeds; season with salt and pepper. Transfer to the oven and roast until the potatoes are golden and cooked through, about 45 minutes. Serve the sausage choucroute with crusty bread and mustard.

Sweet & Sour Pork in Lettuce Cups

Crunchy lettuce cups are perfect for scooping up seasoned ground pork. Serve them as a crowd-pleasing starter or a light, carb-free main course.

TIME	MAKES	CONTRIBUTED BY
30 min total	**4 servings**	**Diane Cu & Todd Porter**

2 Tbsp. canola oil

1 small onion, finely chopped

2 garlic cloves, minced

1 lb. ground pork

2 Tbsp. honey

1 Tbsp. Asian fish sauce

½ tsp. toasted sesame oil

1 tsp. finely grated lime zest plus 2 Tbsp. fresh lime juice

Kosher salt and pepper

1 head of butter lettuce (6 oz.), leaves separated

Thinly sliced scallions, for garnish

Lime wedges, for serving

STEP 1 In a large skillet, heat the canola oil. Add the onion and stir-fry over moderate heat until softened and golden, 5 minutes. Stir in the garlic and cook for 1 minute. Add the pork and cook, stirring occasionally and breaking up the meat, until browned, about 3 minutes. Stir in the honey, fish sauce and sesame oil and cook, stirring, until no traces of pink remain in the pork, about 2 minutes. Remove the skillet from the heat. Stir in the lime zest and lime juice and season with salt and pepper.

STEP 2 Arrange the lettuce cups on a serving platter. Fill with the pork and garnish with scallions. Serve with lime wedges.

Thai-Style Pulled Pork Sandwiches

To make the complex sauce for this pulled pork, Jamie Bissonnette of Toro in New York City mimics an indoor smoker by wrapping all of the spices and aromatics in foil, then cooking the packet directly on the stovetop burner until the contents are charred and pleasantly smoky.

TIME	MAKES	CONTRIBUTED BY
1 hr 15 min active; 5 hr total	**8 to 10 servings**	**Jamie Bissonnette**

⅓ cup Thai red curry paste

¼ cup Asian fish sauce

¼ cup plus 2 Tbsp. finely grated palm sugar or dark brown sugar

One 4-lb. boneless pork shoulder roast with fat cap

Kosher salt and pepper

2 cups chopped cilantro stems

4 garlic cloves

2 large shallots, halved

2 kaffir lime leaves

1 Thai bird chile

1 stalk of fresh lemongrass, inner light green and white parts only, cut into 3 pieces

One ½-inch piece of fresh ginger, peeled and thinly sliced

24 cardamom seeds

1½ tsp. ground turmeric

One 15-oz. can unsweetened coconut milk, chilled

⅓ cup chicken stock or low-sodium broth

½ cup each finely chopped cilantro, Thai basil and mint leaves

Mayonnaise, for spreading

8 brioche buns, split and toasted

Thinly sliced cucumber and red onion, cilantro, Thai basil and lime wedges, for serving

STEP 1 Preheat the oven to 325°. In a small skillet, simmer the curry paste with the fish sauce and ¼ cup of the palm sugar over moderate heat, stirring occasionally, until the sugar is dissolved and a smooth paste forms. Let cool slightly.

STEP 2 Season the pork with salt and rub it all over with the curry paste. Set the roast in a large enameled cast-iron casserole. Cover and roast, basting occasionally with the pan juices, until the meat is very tender, about 3½ hours. Uncover and roast until a golden-brown crust forms, about 15 minutes.

STEP 3 Transfer the pork to a large bowl and let rest for 15 minutes. Using 2 forks, shred the meat. Skim the fat from the pan juices, then stir the juices into the shredded pork. Cover with foil and keep warm.

STEP 4 Make a large double layer of foil. Wrap the cilantro stems, garlic, shallots, lime leaves, chile, lemongrass, ginger, cardamom seeds and turmeric in the foil and seal the sides. Set the packet seam side up directly on a burner or in a cast-iron skillet. Cook over

moderate heat until aromatic and beginning to smoke, 5 minutes. Using tongs, transfer the packet to a rack; let cool slightly. The cilantro stems should be tender and the ingredients on the bottom should be lightly charred.

STEP 5 Scrape the contents of the packet into a food processor. Add the remaining 2 tablespoons of palm sugar and process to a smooth paste.

STEP 6 Open the can of coconut milk and spoon the thick cream on the surface into a large saucepan. Bring to a simmer over moderately high heat and whisk in the cilantro paste. Whisk in the coconut milk and stock and bring to a simmer. Stir in the pulled pork and season with salt and pepper. Cook until the sauce has thickened slightly, about 10 minutes. Stir in the chopped herbs and season with salt and pepper. Keep warm.

STEP 7 Spread mayonnaise on the buns and top with the pulled pork, cucumber, red onion, cilantro and basil leaves. Serve with lime wedges.

ROSÉ

ROSÉ

Over the past decade, dry rosé has transformed from a wine nobody ever wanted to drink to one that stores can't keep in stock. The rash of bad, cheap and sweet White Zinfandel (a rosé, not a white wine) shipped out from California by the jugful in the 1980s and '90s was probably responsible for turning American wine drinkers away from traditional rosé. But thanks to some forward-thinking importers and the pendulum-swing of wine trends, these days "summer water" is one of the fastest-growing categories there is.

The French, especially those who summer on the Mediterranean coast, have always known about the joys of rosé, with Provence setting the bar for what the wine ought to be—light and crisp, with subtle berry and citrus notes, and ideally served outdoors. The best rosés are made with red grapes that are pressed and left on their skins (that's where all the color is) for a short time to achieve the signature pale pink hue. Another (less painstaking) method simply calls for blending red and white wines together.

Today, nearly every winemaking country produces its own version of rosé. Spanish rosados, mostly made in Rioja from Garnacha and Tempranillo, are boldly pink and fruit-forward; German and Austrian rosés, often made from Pinot Noir, tend to be more restrained and refreshing; Argentina's Malbec-based rosados are berry-rich and full-bodied; Californian rosés run the gamut from light Pinot Noir versions to more substantial Cabernet Sauvignon–based ones.

While we have the French to thank for our newfound love affair with all things pink, we also have them to thank for the dishes that these wines best accompany, like seafood stews (bouillabaisse, for instance) or niçoise salads. But the best thing we may have learned from the French is that there's really no specific food or special occasion needed to open a bottle of rosé; kicking back by the grill in the backyard is just as appropriate a setting as sailing on a yacht in Antibes.

Watermelon, Feta & Charred Pepper Salad

Sweet watermelon with creamy feta and salty olives is a classic Mediterranean trio that is utterly addictive. Joseph Ogrodnek and Walker Stern of Battersby in Brooklyn take the combo to the next level with fresh herbs, *gochugaru* (Korean chile flakes) and smoky shishito peppers blistered in a hot skillet. Sprigs of watercress added at the end give the salad an even more peppery bite.

TIME **30 min total**	MAKES **4 to 6 servings**	CONTRIBUTED BY **Joseph Ogrodnek and Walker Stern**

1 lb. seedless watermelon, cut into 1-inch cubes (from one 3¼-lb. watermelon)

2 Kirby cucumbers, peeled and cut into ¾-inch dice

¼ cup very thinly sliced red onion

1½ Tbsp. sherry vinegar

½ tsp. *gochugaru* (Korean red pepper flakes) or Aleppo pepper

¼ cup plus 2 Tbsp. extra-virgin olive oil

Kosher salt and pepper

20 medium shishito peppers (4 oz.)

20 pitted kalamata olives, halved

4 oz. feta cheese, crumbled

1 cup lightly packed watercress leaves

2 Tbsp. minced cilantro

2 Tbsp. finely chopped dill

STEP 1 In a large glass or ceramic baking dish, gently toss the watermelon, cucumbers, red onion, vinegar, *gochugaru* and ¼ cup of the olive oil. Spread in an even layer and season with salt and pepper.

STEP 2 In a large skillet, heat the remaining 2 tablespoons of olive oil until shimmering. Add the shishitos and cook over high heat, tossing, until charred in spots and crisp-tender, about 2 minutes. Transfer the shishitos to the baking dish and toss.

STEP 3 Transfer the salad to plates and garnish with the olives, feta, watercress, cilantro and dill. Serve right away.

WINE TIP

A juicy, warm-climate rosé from Australia or South America will have the substance to stand up to the chile flakes in this salad.

Marinated Olives with Orange

A quick toss in a pan with a mix of orange juice, garlic and spicy crushed red pepper transforms ordinary olives into a sensational cocktail-party home run.

TIME	MAKES	CONTRIBUTED BY
15 min total	**1 quart**	**Martha Wiggins**

2 Tbsp. extra-virgin olive oil

1 Tbsp. thinly sliced garlic

1½ tsp. finely grated orange zest

1 tsp. crushed red pepper

1 qt. mixed olives

⅓ cup fresh orange juice

In a large skillet, heat the oil. Add the garlic, orange zest and crushed red pepper and cook over moderate heat, stirring, until the garlic is softened, 2 minutes. Add the olives and cook, stirring, until hot, 5 minutes. Remove from the heat and stir in the juice. Let cool completely, stirring occasionally. Serve at room temperature.

Soft-Scrambled Eggs with Smoked Sablefish & Trout Roe

NYC chef Andrew Carmellini's luxurious, creamy eggs are heavenly on their own, but serving them with smoky sable, briny roe and sour cream makes them irresistible.

TIME	MAKES	CONTRIBUTED BY
20 min total	**2 servings**	**Andrew Carmellini**

6 large eggs, beaten

¼ cup plus 2 Tbsp. heavy cream

1 Tbsp. unsalted butter

Kosher salt

4 oz. smoked sablefish, sliced ¼ inch thick (see Note)

Trout roe (see Note), thinly sliced scallions and sour cream, for garnish

Toasted sesame, everything or plain bagels, for serving

STEP 1 In a medium nonstick skillet, combine the beaten eggs with the cream and ½ tablespoon of the butter. Cook the eggs over moderately low heat, whisking them constantly, until small curds form and the eggs are creamy, 5 to 7 minutes. Remove the skillet from the heat.

STEP 2 Gently stir the remaining ½ tablespoon of butter into the eggs and season them lightly with salt. Spoon the eggs into 2 serving bowls and top with the sliced sablefish. Garnish with trout roe, sliced scallions and a dollop of sour cream. Serve right away, with toasted bagels.

Note
If smoked sablefish and trout roe are unavailable, smoked salmon and salmon roe can be substituted.

Ham, Leek & Gouda Soufflés

Making a soufflé may seem intimidating—timing it just right can be stressful! But cookbook author Grace Parisi prepares hers in an ingenious make-ahead way that takes the pressure off. She refrigerates the egg yolk base overnight and the next day assembles the individual soufflés up to an hour before baking. Alternatively, the cooked soufflés can be reheated in the oven.

TIME **25 min active; 45 min total**	MAKES **8 servings**	CONTRIBUTED BY **Grace Parisi**

6 Tbsp. unsalted butter, plus softened butter for brushing

¼ cup freshly grated Parmigiano-Reggiano cheese

2 leeks, white parts only, thinly sliced

¼ cup plus 2 Tbsp. all-purpose flour

1½ cups milk

¾ tsp. salt

¼ tsp. cayenne

6 large eggs, separated

5 oz. shredded aged Gouda

6 oz. diced ham

½ tsp. cream of tartar

STEP 1 Preheat the oven to 400° and brush eight 1-cup ramekins with butter. Lightly coat the ramekins with 2 tablespoons of the Parmigiano-Reggiano and set them on a sturdy baking sheet.

STEP 2 In a medium saucepan, melt 2 tablespoons of the butter. Add the leeks and cook over high heat, stirring, just until slightly wilted, about 5 minutes. Transfer to a plate; wipe out the pan. Melt the remaining 4 tablespoons of butter in the saucepan. Whisk in the flour and cook over moderate heat for 1 minute. Whisk in the milk and cook over moderately low heat until smooth and very thick, about 2 minutes. Stir in the salt and cayenne. Off the heat, whisk in the egg yolks. Let cool slightly. Transfer to a large bowl and stir in the Gouda, ham and sautéed leeks.

STEP 3 In a large bowl, using a hand mixer, beat the egg whites with the cream of tartar at medium-high speed until frothy. Increase the speed to high and beat until firm peaks form. With a rubber spatula, fold the egg whites into the soufflé base until no streaks of white remain.

STEP 4 Spoon the soufflé mixture into the prepared ramekins, filling them to ½ inch below the rim. Run your thumb inside the rim of each ramekin to help the soufflés rise evenly. Sprinkle the remaining 2 tablespoons of Parmigiano-Reggiano on top and bake in the bottom third of the oven until the soufflés are puffed and golden brown, 20 minutes. Serve immediately.

Variation

Instead of ramekins, bake in an 8-cup soufflé dish at 375° for 40 minutes.

Ratatouille Toasts with Fried Eggs

Zoe Nathan of Huckleberry in Los Angeles evokes the flavors of southern France with these satisfying toasts loaded with late-summer vegetables. They're an ideal make-ahead brunch recipe; the luscious ratatouille tastes even better when made a day in advance, so the flavors have time to meld. Then all that's left to do is fry the eggs and layer the toasts.

TIME **1 hr active; 1 hr 20 min total**	MAKES **6 servings**	CONTRIBUTED BY **Zoe Nathan**

¾ cup extra-virgin olive oil, plus more for drizzling

3 medium tomatoes, seeded and cut into ½-inch dice (2 cups)

5 garlic cloves

1¼ tsp. crushed red pepper

Kosher salt and black pepper

One 12-oz. eggplant, seeds removed and flesh cut into ½-inch dice (2 cups)

2 small zucchini, cut into ½-inch dice (2 cups)

2 large red onions, cut into ½-inch dice

1 red bell pepper, cut into ½-inch dice

1 bay leaf

1 cup chopped basil, plus more for garnish

6 large eggs

Six ½-inch-thick slices of sourdough bread, toasted

STEP 1 In a large skillet, heat 2 tablespoons of the olive oil. Add the tomatoes, 1 garlic clove and ¼ teaspoon of the crushed red pepper and season with salt. Cook the tomatoes over moderate heat, stirring occasionally, until just softened, about 5 minutes. Scrape the tomatoes into a medium saucepan and discard the garlic clove. Wipe out the skillet. Repeat with the eggplant, zucchini, onions and red bell pepper, cooking each vegetable separately in 2 tablespoons of oil with 1 garlic clove, ¼ teaspoon of crushed red pepper and a generous pinch of salt until just tender and lightly browned, about 7 minutes per vegetable. Add all of the cooked vegetables to the tomatoes in the saucepan.

STEP 2 Add the bay leaf, ½ cup of the chopped basil and ⅓ cup of water to the saucepan with the vegetables. Cover and cook over moderately low heat, stirring occasionally, until the vegetables are very tender, about 20 minutes. Discard the bay leaf and stir in the remaining ½ cup of basil. Season the ratatouille with salt and black pepper and let cool slightly.

STEP 3 Meanwhile, in a large nonstick skillet, heat the remaining 2 tablespoons of olive oil over moderate heat. Crack 3 of the eggs into the skillet and fry until the whites are firm and the yolks are runny, 3 to 5 minutes. Transfer the eggs to a plate, season with salt and pepper and keep warm. Repeat with the remaining 3 eggs.

STEP 4 To serve, spoon the ratatouille onto the toasts and top with the eggs. Drizzle with olive oil and chopped basil and serve.

Prep Ahead
The ratatouille can be refrigerated for up to 3 days. Serve warm or at room temperature.

Sun-Dried Tomato & Arugula Pizza

According to Kenny Rochford of Sonoma's Kosta Browne Winery, the secret to his ultra-crispy pizza crust is giving the dough lots of time to rise so it's pliant enough to stretch very thin. He keeps the toppings minimal: sun-dried tomatoes, fresh mozzarella and arugula.

TIME	MAKES	CONTRIBUTED BY
1 hr active; 2 hr 30 min total	**Eight 8-inch pizzas**	**Kenny Rochford**

DOUGH

4 cups all-purpose flour, plus more for dusting

1 Tbsp. sugar

1 tsp. active dry yeast

1¼ cups warm water

3 Tbsp. extra-virgin olive oil, plus more for greasing

1 tsp. salt

TOPPINGS

32 sun-dried tomato halves (not oil-packed)

4 garlic cloves, chopped

⅓ cup extra-virgin olive oil

1 lb. fresh mozzarella, thinly sliced

Kosher salt and pepper

2 cups packed baby arugula

STEP 1 MAKE THE DOUGH In a stand mixer fitted with the dough hook, mix the 4 cups of flour, the sugar and yeast at medium speed. At low speed, stir in half of the warm water, the 3 tablespoons of olive oil and the salt, then add the remaining water and mix until a ball forms. Mix the dough for 2 minutes at low speed, 2 minutes at medium speed and another 2 minutes at low speed. Transfer the dough to a lightly oiled bowl, cover with plastic wrap and let stand in a warm place until doubled in bulk, about 1½ hours.

STEP 2 Put a pizza stone in the bottom of the oven and heat at 500° for about 45 minutes.

STEP 3 Punch down the dough and scrape it onto a floured work surface. Form the dough into a ball, then cut it into 8 equal pieces. Knead each piece into a ball, then flatten into disks. Cover with plastic wrap and let rest for about 20 minutes.

STEP 4 MEANWHILE, MAKE THE TOPPINGS Put the sun-dried tomatoes in a small saucepan and cover with water. Cover and simmer over low heat until very soft, about 5 minutes. Drain and coarsely chop the tomatoes. In a mini food processor, puree the garlic with the olive oil.

STEP 5 Generously flour a pizza peel. Using a rolling pin, roll out a disk of dough to an 8-inch round, about ⅛ inch thick. (Alternatively, pull and stretch the disk into an 8-inch round.) Transfer the round to the peel and brush with some of the garlic puree. Scatter with one-eighth of the sun-dried tomatoes and arrange one-eighth of the sliced cheese on top. Drizzle with a little more of the garlic puree and season with salt and pepper. Bake on the hot stone for about 4 minutes, until the crust is crisp and the cheese is bubbling. Top with some baby arugula and serve. Repeat with the remaining dough and toppings.

Prep Ahead
The dough can be prepared through Step 1: Punch it down, cover with plastic wrap and refrigerate overnight. The chopped tomatoes and garlic oil can be refrigerated overnight. Bring everything to room temperature before proceeding.

Roast Dorade with Figs, Olives & Almonds

Simple and delicious roast fish is Venice-based blogger Skye McAlpine's go-to dish for lazy weeknights and dinner parties alike. Use the moistest figs you can find so they don't dry out in the oven.

TIME 40 min total	MAKES 4 servings	CONTRIBUTED BY Skye McAlpine

¼ cup extra-virgin olive oil

Four 12-oz. dorade—scaled, cleaned and patted dry

Kosher salt

5 dried Turkish figs, stemmed and quartered

½ cup each pitted Cerignola and Castelvetrano olives

3 Tbsp. rosemary leaves

2 Tbsp. coarsely chopped raw almonds

¼ cup dry white wine

Lemon wedges, for serving

Preheat the oven to 350°. Drizzle 1 tablespoon of the oil in a large roasting pan. Set the dorade in the pan; season generously with salt.

Scatter the figs, olives, rosemary and almonds over and around the fish and drizzle on the wine and remaining 3 tablespoons of oil. Roast for about 30 minutes, until the fish just flakes. Serve with lemon wedges.

Tuna Niçoise Burgers

This fresh tuna burger offers all the sun-drenched flavors of a classic niçoise salad, on a toasted brioche bun.

TIME 30 min total	MAKES 4 servings	CONTRIBUTED BY Grace Parisi

1¼ lbs. fresh tuna, diced

2 scallions, thinly sliced

12 pitted kalamata olives, coarsely chopped

1 Tbsp. salted capers, rinsed and minced

Kosher salt and pepper

Extra-virgin olive oil, for brushing

¼ cup mayonnaise

1½ tsp. anchovy paste

4 brioche buns, split and toasted

Sliced tomatoes and arugula, for serving

STEP 1 Spread the tuna, scallions, olives and capers on a plate and freeze for 5 minutes. Transfer to a food processor and pulse until the tuna is finely chopped. Transfer the mixture to a bowl, season with salt and pepper and form into four 4-inch patties.

STEP 2 Light a grill or heat a grill pan. Brush the burgers with olive oil and grill over moderately high heat, turning once, until golden and crusty and just cooked through, about 6 minutes.

STEP 3 In a small bowl, mix the mayonnaise and anchovy paste; spread on the buns. Top with the burgers, tomato and arugula, close and serve.

Provençal Tuna Sandwiches with Fennel Mayo

WINE TIP Rosé is the classic wine of Provence–the region makes 40 percent of all the rosé in France.

"An afternoon in Malibu with a cooler full of sandwiches and a bottle of rosé, followed by a pinky-orange sunset, is my perfect beach day," says L.A. chef Curtis Stone. One of his favorite sandwiches to pack is this take on pan bagnat, which only gets better as it sits.

TIME **40 min total**	MAKES **4 sandwiches**	CONTRIBUTED BY **Curtis Stone**

2 tsp. fennel seeds

¾ cup mayonnaise

¼ cup crème fraîche

1 garlic clove, finely chopped

1 medium fennel bulb, shaved paper-thin, plus 2 Tbsp. chopped fronds

1 Tbsp. finely grated lemon zest plus 3 Tbsp. fresh lemon juice

Kosher salt and black pepper

¼ cup finely chopped red onion

¼ cup pitted niçoise olives, chopped

2 Tbsp. capers, chopped

1 tsp. crushed red pepper

Two 6-oz. jars tuna packed in olive oil, drained and flaked

2 Tbsp. extra-virgin olive oil

1 baguette, halved lengthwise

2 cups arugula (2 oz.)

2 medium tomatoes, thinly sliced

½ English cucumber, thinly sliced

12 white anchovy fillets

STEP 1 In a small skillet, toast the fennel seeds over moderately low heat until golden, about 3 minutes. Finely crush the seeds in a mortar.

STEP 2 In a food processor, mix the crushed fennel seeds with the mayonnaise, crème fraîche, garlic, fennel fronds, 2 teaspoons of the lemon zest and 1 tablespoon of the lemon juice; puree. Season the fennel mayonnaise with salt and black pepper.

STEP 3 In a medium bowl, mix the onion, olives, capers, crushed red pepper and the remaining 1 teaspoon of lemon zest and 2 tablespoons of lemon juice. Fold in the tuna and extra-virgin olive oil.

STEP 4 Spread the fennel mayo on the cut sides of the baguette. Arrange the arugula on the bottom half of the baguette and top with the shaved fennel and the tuna. Layer the tomatoes, cucumber and anchovies on top. Close the baguette, cut into 4 sandwiches and serve.

Make Ahead

The fennel mayonnaise can be refrigerated for 3 days. The sandwiches can be wrapped in parchment paper and kept in the fridge for 4 hours.

Smoky Paella with Shrimp & Squid

At Jaleo in Washington, DC, José Andrés prepares this classic Spanish rice dish with lots of seafood, including hard-to-find cuttlefish, and a house-made fish stock. To make this equally delicious (and simplified) version at home, replace the cuttlefish with squid and skip the fish stock in favor of bottled clam juice from the supermarket.

TIME	MAKES	CONTRIBUTED BY
45 min total	**4 servings**	**José Andrés**

¼ cup extra-virgin olive oil

1 lb. large shrimp, shelled and deveined

Kosher salt and pepper

1 cup arborio or Valencia rice

1 Tbsp. tomato paste

1 tsp. hot smoked paprika

1 large garlic clove, minced

1 small pinch of saffron, crumbled

2 cups clam juice

½ lb. baby squid, bodies cut into ¼-inch rings

STEP 1 In a large, deep skillet, heat the oil until shimmering. Season the shrimp with salt and pepper and add to the skillet. Cook over high heat until lightly browned on one side, about 2 minutes. Transfer the shrimp to a plate.

STEP 2 Add the rice to the skillet and cook, stirring, until opaque, about 2 minutes. Stir in the tomato paste, paprika, garlic and saffron and cook, stirring, until the rice is toasted and sizzling, about 1 minute. Add the clam juice and 2 cups of water and bring to a boil over high heat. Boil until the rice is still a bit crunchy and about half of the broth is absorbed, about 10 minutes. Lower the heat and simmer until the rice is nearly tender and the liquid is soupy but slightly reduced, about 8 minutes. Stir in the squid, then lay the shrimp on top, cooked side up. Cover and simmer until the squid and shrimp are cooked through and the rice is tender, about 2 minutes longer.

WINE TIP Spanish rosé tends to be darker in hue and fruitier than French ones; it's ideal with seafood main courses like this paella.

Octopus with Chorizo & Potatoes

Chef Alex Larrea of Experimental Beach Ibiza, a restaurant-bar on Spain's "white island," has a smart tip for preparing this traditional dish. He dips the octopus tentacles in hot water three times before cooking, which helps firm them up so they hold their shape. He then simmers the octopus for an hour, until tender, and tosses it with potatoes and smoky, pan-grilled chorizo.

TIME **30 min active; 1 hr 45 min total**	MAKES **4 servings**	CONTRIBUTED BY **Alex Larrea**

1 onion, coarsely chopped

3 bay leaves

1¾ lbs. octopus tentacles

¾ lb. potatoes, peeled and cut into ½-inch dice

Kosher salt and pepper

3 Tbsp. extra-virgin olive oil, plus more for drizzling

2 tsp. chopped thyme

5 oz. cured Spanish chorizo, cut into ½-inch dice

Shredded shiso (optional)

STEP 1 Bring a large saucepan of salted water to a boil with the onion and bay leaves. Using tongs, carefully dip the octopus into the boiling water 3 times, then leave it in the water. Cook the octopus over moderately low heat until tender, about 1 hour. Remove the saucepan from the heat and let the octopus stand in the water for 10 minutes; drain. Cut the octopus into $\frac{1}{2}$-inch pieces.

STEP 2 In a medium saucepan, cover the potatoes with water and add salt. Bring to a boil and simmer over moderate heat until just tender, about 10 minutes. Drain and transfer to a bowl. Toss the potatoes with the 3 tablespoons of olive oil and the thyme; season with salt and pepper.

STEP 3 In a grill pan, cook the chorizo over moderately high heat until warmed through, about 2 minutes. Transfer to a large bowl. Add the potatoes and octopus to the pan and cook until hot and the potatoes are golden in spots, about 5 minutes. Add to the chorizo, season with salt and pepper and toss. Drizzle with oil, garnish with shiso, if using, and serve.

Salmon & Cherry Tomato Skewers with Rosemary Vinaigrette

You can cook these easy kebabs on wooden or metal skewers, but to amp up the flavor, F&W's Justin Chapple sometimes threads them on sturdy rosemary sprigs. The herbs impart a fantastic layer of flavor to the smoky grilled salmon and cherry tomatoes.

TIME **40 min total**	MAKES **4 servings**	CONTRIBUTED BY **Justin Chapple**

¼ cup extra-virgin olive oil, plus more for brushing

3 Tbsp. fresh lemon juice

2 tsp. Dijon mustard

2 tsp. finely chopped rosemary

Kosher salt and pepper

1½ lbs. skinless salmon fillet, cut into 1½-inch cubes

16 cherry tomatoes

4 long metal skewers, or 4 wooden skewers soaked in water for 1 hour

STEP 1 In a small bowl, whisk the ¼ cup of olive oil with the lemon juice, mustard and rosemary. Season the vinaigrette with salt and pepper.

STEP 2 Light a grill or heat a grill pan. Thread the salmon and cherry tomatoes onto the skewers, brush with olive oil and season all over with salt and pepper. Grill over moderately high heat, turning once, until the salmon is just cooked through, about 6 minutes. Transfer the skewers to a platter and drizzle with some of the vinaigrette. Serve right away, passing additional vinaigrette at the table.

WINE TIP

The juicy, melony style of rosé that's common in California is a terrific match for many types of grilled foods, and salmon is no exception.

Chicken with Piquillos

Mario Batali learned to make this luscious braised chicken dish in a rich white wine and pepper sauce while filming the PBS series *Spain...On the Road Again.* Pilar Sanchez, a seasoned home cook from Asturias, in the country's northwest, taught him how to make the local specialty. When Batali asked where she buys her poultry, Sanchez told him to go to her yard and listen for the "singing in the field" from the chickens she raises.

TIME	MAKES	CONTRIBUTED BY
35 min active; 2 hr 15 min total	**4 servings**	**Mario Batali**

One 3½-lb. chicken, cut into 8 pieces

2 garlic cloves, sliced

Kosher salt

2 Tbsp. extra-virgin olive oil

1 large onion, coarsely chopped

One 9-oz. jar piquillo peppers, drained

1 cup dry white wine

STEP 1 Rub the chicken with the garlic and 1 tablespoon of salt. Cover and refrigerate for 1 hour.

STEP 2 Heat the olive oil in a large, deep skillet. Scrape the garlic off the chicken pieces. Add the chicken to the skillet in a single layer and cook over moderately high heat, turning occasionally, until browned all over, about 12 minutes. Transfer the chicken to a platter.

STEP 3 Add the onion to the skillet and cook over low heat, stirring occasionally, until very tender, about 10 minutes. Add the piquillo peppers and white wine and bring to a simmer, scraping up any browned bits.

STEP 4 Return the chicken and any accumulated juices to the skillet. Cover partially and cook over low heat until the chicken is tender and cooked through and the sauce is thickened, about 30 minutes. Transfer the chicken to a platter, spoon the sauce on top and serve.

Make Ahead
The chicken can be refrigerated overnight; rewarm before serving.

Smoked-Duck Salad with Walnuts & Raspberries

The traditional flavors of southwestern France—meaty duck breasts, duck cracklings, toasted walnuts and walnut oil—combine beautifully with sweet, tangy raspberries and slightly bitter frisée. Cookbook author Marcia Kiesel created this completely original salad to pair with a lightly fruity Bordeaux rosé.

TIME	MAKES	CONTRIBUTED BY
30 min total	**4 servings**	**Marcia Kiesel**

½ lb. smoked duck breast—skin and fat removed and reserved, breast thinly sliced crosswise

½ cup walnuts

2 Tbsp. sherry vinegar

2½ tsp. Dijon mustard

1 small shallot, very finely chopped

3 Tbsp. walnut oil

1 Tbsp. vegetable oil

Kosher salt and pepper

6 oz. frisée, torn into bite-size pieces (6 cups)

3 cups packed torn Boston lettuce

1 cup raspberries

STEP 1 Preheat the oven to 350°. Spread the duck skin and fat in a pie plate and bake for about 15 minutes, until crisp. Drain the cracklings on paper towels, then break into pieces.

STEP 2 Meanwhile, spread the walnuts in a pie plate and toast until fragrant, about 8 minutes. Let cool, then coarsely chop the nuts.

STEP 3 In a large bowl, mix the vinegar with the mustard and shallot. Gradually whisk in the walnut and vegetable oils. Season generously with salt and pepper. Add the frisée, Boston lettuce and walnuts and toss to coat. Top the salad with the raspberries, sliced duck breast and cracklings and serve.

WINE TIP
More and more Bordeaux properties—even top châteaus—have started making rosé as the popularity of the category continues to grow.

Sausages with Peaches & Pickled Chiles

This super-simple grilled dish calls for just a few elements, so Tandy Wilson of Nashville's City House insists that you use the best peaches you can find. The sliced fruit adds a pleasantly sweet and fresh contrast to the spicy sausages and tangy pickled jalapeños.

TIME **30 min active; 1 hr 30 min total**	MAKES **4 servings**	CONTRIBUTED BY **Tandy Wilson**

¼ cup apple cider vinegar

¼ cup distilled white vinegar

3 Tbsp. sorghum syrup or molasses

1½ tsp. kosher salt

2 jalapeños, seeded and thinly sliced

1 small red onion, thinly sliced

Canola oil, for brushing

Six 4-oz. hot Italian sausages

2 medium peaches, pitted and sliced ¼ inch thick

STEP 1 In a 1-quart jar, shake the apple cider and distilled white vinegars with the sorghum syrup, salt and ½ cup of water until the salt dissolves. Add the jalapeños and onion, cover and let stand at room temperature for at least 1 hour.

STEP 2 Light a grill and oil the grate. Grill the sausages over moderate heat, turning, until lightly charred and cooked through, 10 to 12 minutes. Transfer to a cutting board and let rest for 5 minutes, then thinly slice on the diagonal.

STEP 3 Arrange the sliced peaches on a platter. Top with the sausages and some of the pickled jalapeños and onion. Drizzle with some of the pickling liquid and serve the remaining pickles on the side.

Prep Ahead
The drained pickles can be refrigerated for up to 1 week.

REDS

VARIETALS

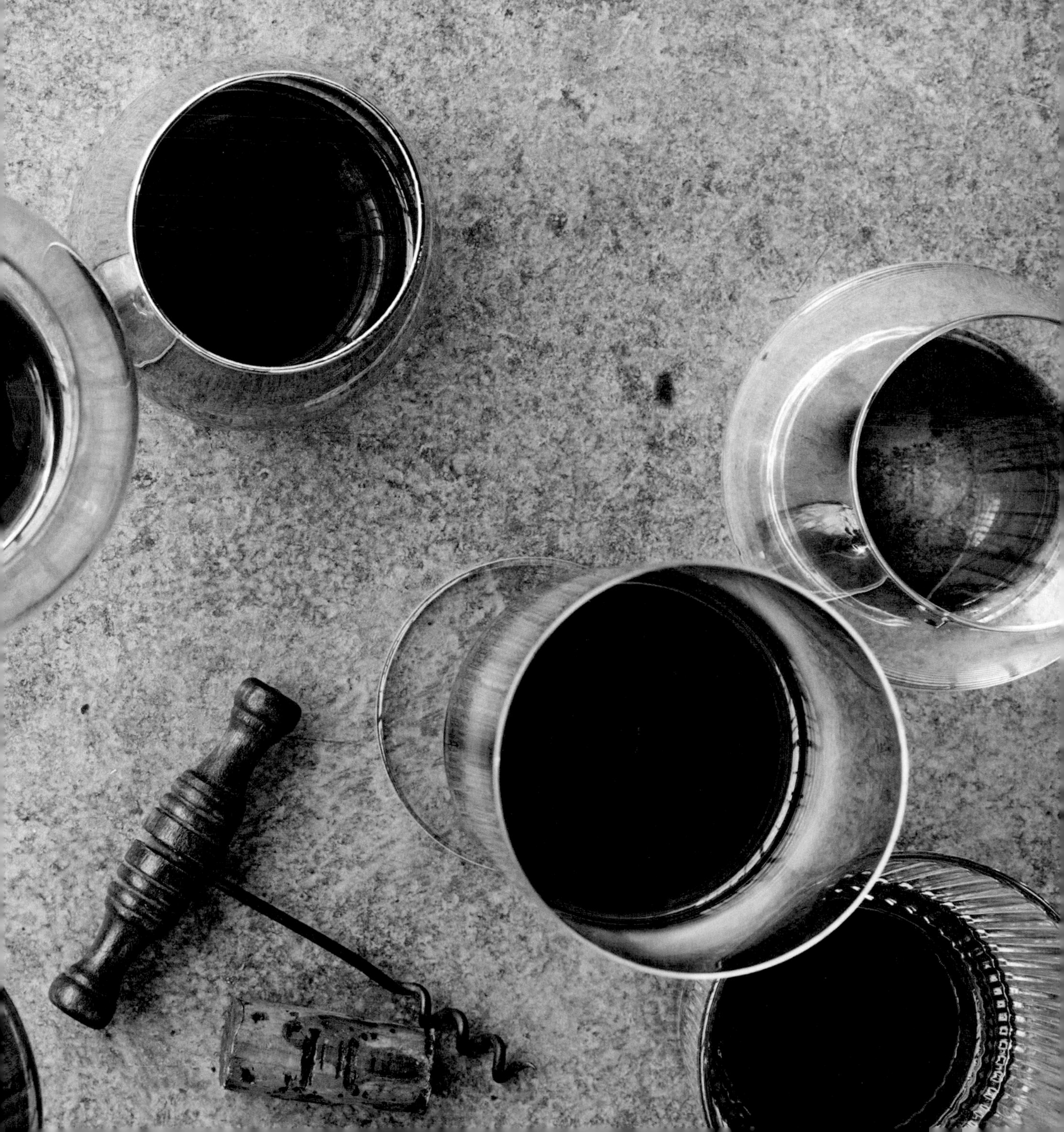

PINOT NOIR
& OTHER SAVORY, AROMATIC REDS

PINOT NOIR No grape is more romanticized than Pinot Noir. Great red Burgundies (which are made from Pinot Noir) impressively blur the aromatic line between fruit and earth, distinctly express the character of the vineyards they're from and unfold almost magically when given enough time in a cellar. People reach for poetry when describing them (for better or worse), pulling out evocative words like "savory," "forest floor" or "Darjeeling tea." In line with those expectations, every tiny parcel of Burgundy has a name, with vineyards exactingly subdivided into rigid levels of quality: village, premier cru, grand cru.

While every winemaker who works with Pinot Noir outside of Burgundy will admit that it's impossible to replicate those wines, the nuance and depth of expression offered by Pinot Noir grown in Burgundy is always the goal. That means, in every region where it's grown, a lot of effort goes into making Pinot—and it's not an easy grape to deal with. Pinot Noir is thin-skinned and demands exceptional care in the vineyards. It also requires a cool climate, limiting great Pinot Noir to regions like the Sonoma Coast and parts of Santa Barbara County in California, the Willamette Valley in Oregon and the cooler parts of New Zealand. As in Burgundy, certain vineyards have emerged within each of these regions as exceptional places to grow Pinot.

But overall, in California the wines tend to display more generous fruit than savory red Burgundies do. Oregon versions are more spicy and streamlined; in New Zealand, the best Pinots balance juicy berry fruit with distinctive earthy notes.

Sommeliers love Pinot Noir for its versatility with food: It pairs as well with earthy mushroom dishes as it does with roasted meat and duck and richer fish like salmon or monkfish.

GAMAY Gamay is the grape of Beaujolais, in the very southern part of Burgundy. Beaujolais often plays kid brother to red Burgundy, but it's a simpler wine—more accessible at an earlier age, less problematic in the vineyard and more affordable, too. The region is divided into 10 different crus: Brouilly, Côte de Brouilly, Régnié, Juliénas, Morgon, St-Amour, Chénas, Moulin-à-Vent, Fleurie and Chiroubles, each of which has its own personality. Gamay produces light- to medium-bodied wines with vibrant red and dark fruit, subtle earth notes and impressive acidity. Those qualities make them able to pair with just about anything, from seafood to steak. Beaujolais's popularity among sommeliers and winemakers in the US has encouraged some growers in the States to try their hand with Gamay, too. Thus far, Oregon's Willamette Valley is seeing the most success, with wines that are exuberant and fresh.

NEBBIOLO The king and queen of Italy's Piedmont region, Barolo and Barbaresco are made from exactly the same grape variety, Nebbiolo. Named for the fog (*nebbia*) that regularly envelops the Piedmontese hills, Nebbiolo produces some of the most nuanced wines made in Italy. Often compared to Pinot Noir from Burgundy, Nebbiolo is in fact a vastly different grape. Whereas Pinot is relatively low in tannins, Nebbiolo is firmly tannic, which means that a majority of the wines made from it are tense and astringent when young. Barolo, in particular, demands time in the bottle to smooth out; Barbaresco can be a bit more approachable early on. One similarity that Barolo and Barbaresco do share with Burgundy is that, thanks to a diverse geology, the wines are markedly different from one vineyard to the next.

Nebbiolos from outside these lauded regions, in Piedmont's greater Langhe area as well as Valtellina and the Valle d'Aosta, are often ready to drink much sooner (they're also dramatically more affordable). At their pinnacle, wines made from Nebbiolo offer layers of flavor: earth, red fruits, alluring spice and floral aromas, all bolstered by a youthful acidity that sustains regardless of the wine's age. Serve Nebbiolos with roasts, game birds and tomato-based pastas, or anything involving Piedmont's other famous product, truffles.

Spaghetti with Mushroom Bolognese

WINE
TIP

Pinot Noir's earthy notes are a perfect foil for the equally earthy, umami-rich character of mushrooms.

Three kinds of mushrooms plus eggplant and carrots come together in this ultra-satisfying meatless take on pasta Bolognese. Miso is the secret ingredient that adds extra seasoning and depth of flavor to the sauce.

TIME **1 hr active; 2 hr 30 min total**	MAKES **4 servings**	CONTRIBUTED BY **Kay Chun**

¼ cup dried porcini mushrooms

¼ cup plus 2 Tbsp. extra-virgin olive oil

1 small onion, cut into ¼-inch dice

2 medium carrots, peeled and cut into ¼-inch dice

1 baby eggplant (8 oz.), peeled and cut into ¼-inch dice

1 lb. cremini mushrooms, one-fourth sliced, the rest cut into ¼-inch dice

8 oz. shiitake mushrooms, stemmed, caps cut into ¼-inch dice

Kosher salt and pepper

5 garlic cloves, minced

2 Tbsp. tomato paste

1 Tbsp. shiro (white) miso

One 2-inch chunk of Parmigiano-Reggiano cheese, plus grated cheese for serving

One 28-oz. can whole peeled tomatoes, crushed

1 thyme sprig

½ tsp. turbinado sugar

¾ lb. spaghetti

2 Tbsp. chopped parsley

STEP 1 In a small bowl, cover the porcini with 1 cup of boiling water; soak until softened, about 30 minutes. Finely chop the porcini, discarding any tough bits. Pour off and reserve ½ cup of the soaking liquid.

STEP 2 In a large enameled cast-iron casserole, heat 2 tablespoons of the oil. Add the onion and carrots and cook over moderate heat until light golden, about 8 minutes. Add the eggplant and 2 tablespoons of the oil and cook, stirring occasionally, until softened, 8 minutes. Stir in the cremini, shiitake, chopped porcini and the remaining 2 tablespoons of oil and season with salt and pepper. Cook, stirring occasionally, until the mushrooms are golden, 8 to 10 minutes. Stir in the garlic, tomato paste and miso and cook for 2 minutes. Add the chunk of cheese, the tomatoes and their juices, the thyme, sugar and reserved mushroom soaking liquid and bring to a simmer.

STEP 3 Cover the casserole and cook over low heat, stirring occasionally, until the sauce is very thick, about 1½ hours. Discard the thyme sprig; season the sauce with salt and pepper.

STEP 4 In a pot of salted boiling water, cook the spaghetti until al dente. Drain, reserving ¼ cup of the pasta water.

STEP 5 Add the pasta, pasta water and parsley to the sauce; toss to coat. Serve in bowls, topped with grated cheese.

Make Ahead
The mushroom Bolognese can be refrigerated for up to 2 days.

Leek & Mushroom Croquettes

At Poppy in Seattle, Jerry Traunfeld flavors his crisp, creamy-centered, walnut-size croquettes with dried porcini. This simpler recipe uses easier-to-find fresh shiitake (which don't need to be soaked) and makes the croquettes larger for a completely satisfying vegetarian main course.

TIME	MAKES	CONTRIBUTED BY
40 min active; 3 hr total	**12 croquettes**	**Jerry Traunfeld**

5 Tbsp. unsalted butter

2 leeks, white and tender green parts only, thinly sliced

¼ lb. shiitake mushrooms, stemmed, caps thinly sliced

Kosher salt and pepper

1 tsp. chopped thyme

1 tsp. chopped oregano

3 Tbsp. all-purpose flour, plus more for coating

1 cup milk

½ cup shredded Gruyère cheese

¼ cup freshly grated Parmigiano-Reggiano cheese

2 large eggs beaten with 2 Tbsp. water

1½ cups panko

Vegetable oil, for frying

STEP 1 In a large skillet, melt 2 tablespoons of the butter. Add the leeks and shiitake, season with salt and pepper and cook over high heat, stirring frequently, until the leeks and mushrooms are softened and beginning to brown, about 7 minutes. Add the thyme and oregano to the vegetables and transfer to a medium bowl.

STEP 2 In a small saucepan, melt the remaining 3 tablespoons of butter. Whisk in the 3 tablespoons of flour and cook over high heat until bubbling, 1 minute. Add the milk and cook, whisking, until very thick and bubbling, about 3 minutes. Scrape the mixture into the bowl. Add the Gruyère and Parmigiano-Reggiano, season with salt and pepper and stir until the mixture is evenly combined.

STEP 3 Lay an 18-inch-long piece of plastic wrap on a work surface. Spoon the croquette mixture onto the plastic in a 12-inch strip. Roll up the plastic, pressing the croquette mixture into a 14-inch log, and twist the ends. Freeze the croquette log until very firm, about 2 hours.

STEP 4 Fill 3 shallow bowls with flour, the beaten eggs and the panko and line a large baking sheet with wax paper. Unwrap the log and cut the croquette mixture into 12 pieces. Using floured hands, pat each piece into a 2-inch round patty, about ¾ inch thick. Dredge each patty in the flour, then dip in the eggs and coat with panko, pressing to help it adhere. Set the croquettes on the baking sheet and freeze for 15 minutes.

STEP 5 In a large skillet, heat ½ inch of oil to 375°. Add all of the croquettes and fry over high heat, turning once or twice, until they are golden and crisp, about 5 minutes. Drain on paper towels and serve hot.

Prep Ahead
The leek-mushroom croquettes can be prepared through Step 3 and refrigerated overnight.

Carrot Osso Buco

WINE TIP Porcini powder and mushroom broth provide umami notes that call for a savory red.

Top Chef judge Richard Blais creates a playful vegan riff on osso buco by braising very large pieces of carrots (instead of veal shanks) until spoon-tender. Even without the shanks, the dish has a meaty, umami-rich flavor thanks to ground dried porcini mushrooms in the sauce.

TIME **30 min active; 1 hr 50 min total**	MAKES **4 servings**	CONTRIBUTED BY **Richard Blais**

½ lb. red pearl onions

1 Tbsp. plus 1 tsp. vegetable oil

3 very large carrots, cut crosswise 1 inch thick at the wide ends and 1½ inches thick toward the narrow ends

Kosher salt and pepper

1 tsp. curry powder

1 cup dry red wine

1 Tbsp. porcini mushroom powder (ground dried porcini mushrooms)

1½ cups prepared mushroom broth

½ cup flat-leaf parsley leaves

2 tsp. fresh lemon juice

STEP 1 Preheat the oven to 350°. In a large, deep ovenproof skillet, bring 1 inch of water to a boil. Add the pearl onions and cook for 1 minute. Drain and trim the onions, then peel them. Wipe out the skillet.

STEP 2 Return the skillet to the heat and add 1 tablespoon of the oil. Add the carrots in a single layer, season with salt and pepper and cook over moderate heat, turning, until browned, about 5 minutes per side. Add the pearl onions, sprinkle with the curry powder and cook, stirring a few times, until fragrant, about 1 minute. Add the wine and simmer over moderately high heat for 3 minutes. Add the porcini powder and mushroom broth and bring to a boil. Transfer the skillet to the oven and braise the carrots for 1 hour and 15 minutes, turning once, until tender.

STEP 3 Season the sauce with salt and pepper. Spoon the carrots, onions and sauce into shallow bowls. In a small bowl, toss the parsley with the lemon juice and the remaining 1 teaspoon of oil and season with salt and pepper. Scatter the parsley leaves over the carrots and serve.

Make Ahead
The carrot osso buco can be refrigerated overnight. Reheat gently.

Serve With
Soft polenta or celery root puree.

Crusty Baked Shells & Cauliflower

Sautéed cauliflower gets the decadant treatment in this cheesy baked pasta from Food Network star Ina Garten. She mixes in Italian Fontina Val d'Aosta, which is super nutty and melts beautifully. Sage, capers and garlic add even more pops of flavor. Be sure to boil your pasta just until al dente, as you don't want it to overcook in the oven.

TIME	MAKES	CONTRIBUTED BY
1 hr active; 1 hr 30 min total	**6 to 8 servings**	**Ina Garten**

Kosher salt and freshly ground black pepper

¾ lb. medium shells, such as Barilla

Good olive oil

2½ lbs. cauliflower, cut into small florets (1 large head)

3 Tbsp. roughly chopped fresh sage leaves

2 Tbsp. capers, drained

1 Tbsp. minced garlic (3 cloves)

½ tsp. grated lemon zest

¼ tsp. crushed red pepper flakes

2 cups freshly grated Italian Fontina Val d'Aosta cheese, lightly packed (10 oz. with rind)

1 cup (8 oz.) fresh ricotta

½ cup panko (Japanese bread flakes)

6 Tbsp. freshly grated Italian Pecorino cheese

2 Tbsp. minced fresh parsley leaves

STEP 1 Preheat the oven to 400°.

STEP 2 Fill a large pot with water, add 2 tablespoons of salt and bring to a boil. Add the pasta and cook until al dente, according to the instructions on the package. Since it will be baked later, don't overcook it! Drain and pour into a very large bowl.

STEP 3 Meanwhile, heat 3 tablespoons of olive oil in a large (12-inch) sauté pan over medium-high heat, add half of the cauliflower in one layer and sauté for 5 to 6 minutes, tossing occasionally, until the florets are lightly browned and tender. Pour the cauliflower, including the small bits, into the bowl with the pasta. Add 3 more tablespoons of olive oil to the sauté pan, add the remaining cauliflower, cook until browned and tender and add to the bowl.

STEP 4 Add the sage, capers, garlic, lemon zest, red pepper flakes, 2 teaspoons salt and 1 teaspoon black pepper to the bowl and stir carefully. Stir in the Fontina. Transfer half of the mixture to a 10 x 13 x 2-inch rectangular baking dish. Spoon rounded tablespoons of ricotta on the pasta and spoon the remaining pasta mixture on top. Combine the panko, Pecorino, parsley and 1 tablespoon of olive oil in a small bowl and sprinkle it evenly on top. Bake for 25 to 30 minutes, until browned and crusty on top. Serve hot.

Prep Ahead

Assemble the dish, cover and refrigerate overnight. Bake before serving.

Lentil & Smoky Eggplant Stew

While you could make this stew with any kind of lentil, Fernanda Milanezi of Jamies Wine Bar in London prefers the small, almost round French green du Puy lentils. The advantage is that they hold their shape nicely even when fully cooked.

TIME	MAKES	CONTRIBUTED BY
20 min active; 1 hr 30 min total	**12 servings**	**Fernanda Milanezi**

¼ cup extra-virgin olive oil, plus more for drizzling

1 medium onion, finely chopped

1 celery rib, finely chopped

5 garlic cloves, finely chopped

1 bay leaf

3 cups French green du Puy lentils (20 oz.), rinsed and picked over

1 can (14.5 oz.) chopped tomatoes

2 qts. vegetable stock

2 medium eggplants (1½ lbs.)

2 Tbsp. harissa

⅓ cup chopped parsley

Kosher salt and pepper

Greek yogurt, chopped walnuts and parsley, small mint leaves and pomegranate molasses, for serving

STEP 1 Preheat the broiler. In a large saucepan, heat 2 tablespoons of the oil. Add the onion, celery, garlic and bay leaf and cook over moderate heat until softened. Add the lentils, tomatoes and stock; bring to a simmer over moderately high heat. Cover, reduce the heat and simmer, stirring occasionally, until the lentils are tender but still hold their shape, about 45 minutes. Discard the bay leaf.

STEP 2 Meanwhile, set the eggplants on a foil-lined baking sheet and rub with the remaining 2 tablespoons of olive oil. Broil 6 inches from the heat, turning occasionally, until completely blackened and tender, about 20 minutes. Let cool.

STEP 3 Cut the eggplants in half lengthwise and scoop the flesh into a colander set over a bowl; discard the skins. Let the eggplant drain for 5 minutes, then transfer to a bowl and mash until smooth.

STEP 4 Stir the harissa and half of the roasted eggplant into the lentils until warmed through. Stir in the ⅓ cup of chopped parsley and season with salt and pepper. Ladle the stew into bowls; top with the remaining eggplant. Garnish with yogurt, walnuts, parsley and mint. Add a drizzle of pomegranate molasses and olive oil and serve.

Poulet Basquaise with Currant Couscous

This hearty, slow-braised chicken with peppers and tomatoes is a standout among the French country dishes that Shawn Gawle served at (the now-shuttered) Les Clos wine bar in San Francisco. The sauce is enhanced with smoky Spanish paprika and a splash of sherry vinegar.

TIME **1 hr 15 min active; 2 hr 30 min total**	MAKES **4 servings**	CONTRIBUTED BY **Shawn Gawle**

CHICKEN

2 Tbsp. canola oil

6 whole chicken legs, separated into thighs and drumsticks

Kosher salt and pepper

1 small red onion, minced

1 poblano chile, chopped

1 red bell pepper, chopped

1 lb. tomatoes, chopped

1 tsp. pimentón de la Vera

½ cup dry white wine

2 Tbsp. sherry vinegar

3 thyme sprigs

2 bay leaves

COUSCOUS

1 cup dry white wine

¼ cup plus 2 Tbsp. extra-virgin olive oil

Small pinch of saffron threads

2½ cups couscous (about 14 oz.)

½ cup dried currants

¼ cup minced red onion

1 tsp. kosher salt

STEP 1 MAKE THE CHICKEN
Preheat the oven to 350°. In a large enameled cast-iron casserole, heat the oil. Season the chicken with salt and pepper. Add half of the pieces to the casserole and cook over moderately high heat until browned all over, about 8 minutes. Transfer to a plate. Brown the remaining chicken.

STEP 2 Pour off all but 2 tablespoons of the oil from the casserole. Add the onion, poblano and bell pepper. Cook over moderate heat, stirring, until softened, 8 to 10 minutes. Stir in the tomatoes and cook until broken down, about 8 minutes. Add the pimentón and cook for 1 minute. Add the wine, vinegar, thyme and bay leaves and simmer until the liquid is reduced by half, about 2 minutes. Nestle the chicken pieces in the sauce, cover and braise in the oven until cooked through, about 1 hour and 15 minutes; discard the thyme sprigs and bay leaves.

STEP 3 MAKE THE COUSCOUS
In a medium saucepan, combine the wine, oil, saffron and 1 cup of water and bring to a boil. In a large heatproof bowl, combine the couscous, currants, onion and salt. Pour the hot wine mixture over, cover and let stand until the couscous is tender and the liquid is absorbed, about 30 minutes. Fluff the couscous and serve with the chicken.

Chicken Legs Coq au Vin

At NYC's Aldo Sohm Wine Bar, Eric Ripert creates casual French food to go with the accessible bottles on the wine list. For his coq au vin—typically made with a cut-up chicken—he uses only drumsticks, so the meat cooks uniformly. He suggests using a wine for the sauce that's similar to what's being paired with the dish so the flavors are seamless.

TIME	MAKES	CONTRIBUTED BY
45 min active; 2 hr 15 min total	**4 servings**	**Eric Ripert**

8 chicken drumsticks (2 lbs.)

Kosher salt and pepper

3 Tbsp. all-purpose flour

2 Tbsp. canola oil

1 slice of bacon, chopped (optional)

½ cup finely chopped carrot

½ cup finely chopped onion

½ cup finely chopped celery

1½ cups chopped mushrooms (3 oz.)

2 garlic cloves, thinly sliced

½ cup brandy

1 Tbsp. tomato paste

1 bottle dry red wine

1 cup chicken stock

2 thyme sprigs, plus chopped thyme for garnish

STEP 1 Season the chicken with salt and pepper and dust all over with 2 tablespoons of the flour. In a large cast-iron casserole, heat the oil. Add the chicken and cook over moderately high heat, turning, until golden, about 5 minutes. Transfer to a plate.

STEP 2 Add the bacon to the casserole and cook until crisp, 1 to 2 minutes. Add the carrot, onion, celery, mushrooms and garlic and cook over moderate heat, stirring, until golden, about 5 minutes. Stir in the brandy and cook until reduced by half, about 1 minute. Stir in the tomato paste and the remaining 1 tablespoon of flour until incorporated. Add the wine, stock and thyme sprigs; bring to a boil. Return the chicken to the pot and bring to a simmer. Cover and cook over low heat, turning the chicken occasionally, until very tender, about 1½ hours. Transfer the chicken to a plate.

STEP 3 Simmer the sauce until thickened and reduced by half, about 10 minutes. Season with salt and pepper and discard the thyme sprigs. Return the chicken to the sauce and heat through. Garnish with chopped thyme and serve.

Make Ahead
The coq au vin can be refrigerated for up to 3 days.

Curry Fried Chicken Wings

WINE TIP

People tend to default to off-dry whites with curry-flavored dishes, but aromatic, light-bodied reds pair very well, too.

Bryant Ng, chef at Cassia in Los Angeles, gives these succulent chicken wings an irresistibly crisp coating with panko and cornstarch; curry powder in the marinade and the crust provides a one-two punch of flavor.

TIME **45 min, plus overnight marinating**	MAKES **4 to 6 servings**	CONTRIBUTED BY **Bryant Ng**

2 lbs. chicken wings, cut into 2 pieces at the joints

2 Tbsp. Madras curry powder

Kosher salt

6 garlic cloves, crushed

¼ cup coconut vinegar (see Note) or unseasoned rice vinegar

1 Tbsp. Asian fish sauce

1 cup cornstarch

2 large eggs, lightly beaten

2 Tbsp. unsweetened coconut milk

2 cups all-purpose flour

1 cup panko, finely crushed

2 tsp. cayenne

2 tsp. freshly ground white pepper

2 tsp. freshly ground black pepper

Vegetable oil, for frying

Lime wedges, for serving

STEP 1 In a shallow baking dish, toss the chicken wings with 1 tablespoon of the curry powder and 2 teaspoons of salt; arrange the wings in a single layer. Nestle the crushed garlic cloves around the wings and drizzle the vinegar and fish sauce over them. Cover and refrigerate overnight.

STEP 2 Spread the cornstarch in a pie plate and season with 1 teaspoon of salt. In another pie plate, whisk the eggs with the coconut milk. In a large bowl, whisk the flour with the panko, cayenne, white and black pepper, 1 teaspoon of salt and the remaining 1 tablespoon of curry powder.

STEP 3 Line a baking sheet with wax paper. Working in batches, dredge the wings in the cornstarch and shake off the excess, then dip them in the egg mixture and coat thoroughly with the panko flour. Transfer the wings to the baking sheet.

STEP 4 In a large saucepan, heat 2 inches of oil to 350°. Add half of the wings and fry over moderate heat, turning once, until deep golden brown and cooked through, about 8 minutes. Transfer the wings to paper towels to drain and fry the remaining wings. Serve with lime wedges.

Note
Coconut vinegar is a low-acid vinegar made from the sap of coconut trees. It is available at health food stores and online.

Sesame-Ginger Chicken Meatballs

These super-quick, juicy little Asian-inspired meatballs are terrific served with steamed rice, in lettuce cups or on their own as hors d'oeuvres.

TIME **30 min total**	MAKES **4 servings**	CONTRIBUTED BY **Justin Chapple**

Canola oil, for brushing

1 lb. ground chicken, preferably dark meat

½ cup plain dry breadcrumbs

⅓ cup minced scallions, plus thinly sliced scallions for garnish

3 Tbsp. minced peeled fresh ginger

1 large egg

2 garlic cloves, minced

2 tsp. toasted sesame oil

2 tsp. soy sauce

¼ tsp. kosher salt

Asian chile sauce, for serving

Preheat the oven to 450° and brush a rimmed baking sheet with canola oil. In a large bowl, mix together all of the remaining ingredients except the sliced scallions and chile sauce. Form the mixture into 1½-inch balls and arrange them on the baking sheet. Brush the meatballs with canola oil and bake until browned and cooked through, 13 minutes. Transfer the meatballs to a platter, garnish with sliced scallions and serve with Asian chile sauce.

Roast Chicken with 40 Brussels Sprouts

In this cheeky take on James Beard's chicken with 40 cloves of garlic, brussels sprouts absorb the fantastic flavor of the caraway-infused chicken juices in the pan.

TIME **10 min active; 1 hr 15 min total**	MAKES **4 servings**	CONTRIBUTED BY **Kay Chun**

One 4-lb. chicken

2 Tbsp. extra-virgin olive oil

Kosher salt and pepper

40 brussels sprouts, trimmed

2 Tbsp. unsalted butter, cubed

1 tsp. caraway seeds

2 Tbsp. fresh lemon juice, plus wedges for serving

Preheat the oven to 450°. Rub the chicken with the olive oil and season with salt and pepper. Place the chicken in a roasting pan and roast for 30 minutes. Add the brussels sprouts, butter and caraway seeds to the pan and roast for 20 minutes longer, until an instant-read thermometer inserted in the inner thighs registers 165°. Sprinkle the lemon juice over the sprouts and let the chicken rest for 15 minutes. Carve the chicken, toss the brussels sprouts and serve with lemon wedges.

Duck Confit & White Bean Stew

WINE TIP

For duck, red Burgundy is a classic partner, especially with a French-influenced dish like this one.

Erin French of The Lost Kitchen in Freedom, Maine, created this easy three-step take on the usually laborious Gallic classic known as cassoulet. She confits ducks raised by a local friend, but to save time, start with duck leg confit, which you can buy online from dartagnan.com. Radicchio stirred in at the end adds a fresh bite.

TIME **45 min active; 1 hr 45 min total, plus overnight soaking**	MAKES **8 servings**	CONTRIBUTED BY **Erin French**

2 qts. low-sodium chicken broth

2 cups dried cannellini beans (¾ lb.), soaked overnight and drained

2 Tbsp. extra-virgin olive oil

Four 6-oz. whole confit duck legs

6 large shallots, thinly sliced

4 purple or orange carrots, sliced ¼ inch thick

2 garlic cloves, crushed

2 thyme sprigs, plus leaves for serving

1 tsp. herbes de Provence

1 small head of radicchio, leaves torn into bite-size pieces

STEP 1 In a large pot, combine the chicken broth and beans with 4 cups of water and bring to a boil. Simmer over moderate heat until the beans are tender, about 1 hour.

STEP 2 Meanwhile, in a large skillet, heat the olive oil. Add the duck legs and cook over moderate heat, turning occasionally, until crisp and heated through, about 15 minutes. Transfer to a plate to cool slightly, then coarsely chop or shred the meat. Set aside the crispy skin.

STEP 3 Add the shallots, carrots, garlic, thyme sprigs and herbes de Provence to the skillet and cook over moderate heat, stirring occasionally, until the shallots are caramelized and completely tender, about 20 minutes. Add 2 tablespoons of water to the skillet and stir, scraping up any browned bits. Discard the thyme sprigs. Stir the shallots and carrots into the beans, then stir in the duck and radicchio. Garnish with thyme leaves and serve topped with the crispy skin.

Prep Ahead
The stew (without the radicchio) can be refrigerated for up to 2 days. Reheat gently and add the radicchio just before serving.

Duck Breasts with Mustard & Candied Kumquats

This spicy, tangy sauce is a great complement to seared duck breasts. It blends fiery mustard and jalapeño with candied kumquats, tiny citrus fruits with a sweet-tart flavor somewhere between a tangerine and a lime.

TIME **25 min active; 1 hr total**	MAKES **4 servings**	CONTRIBUTED BY **Marcia Kiesel**

½ cup dry white wine

1 Tbsp. plus 1 tsp. pure olive oil

1½ tsp. grainy mustard

1 tsp. chopped rosemary

Four ½-lb. duck breasts, skin and fat removed

6 oz. kumquats, sliced crosswise ⅓ inch thick

½ cup sugar

Kosher salt and pepper

2 medium shallots, thinly sliced

1 jalapeño, seeded and thinly sliced

1 Tbsp. Dijon mustard

STEP 1 In a shallow dish, combine the wine with 1 teaspoon of the olive oil and ½ teaspoon each of the grainy mustard and rosemary. Add the duck breasts and turn to coat. Cover and refrigerate for 30 minutes.

STEP 2 Meanwhile, bring a medium saucepan of water to a boil. Add the kumquat slices and simmer over moderately high heat until tender, about 5 minutes. Drain the kumquat slices. In the same saucepan, combine the sugar and ½ cup of water and bring to a boil, stirring to dissolve the sugar. Add the kumquat slices and simmer over moderate heat for 8 minutes. Transfer the kumquats and sugar syrup to a heatproof bowl.

STEP 3 In a large skillet, heat the remaining 1 tablespoon of olive oil. Remove the duck breasts from the marinade; reserve the marinade. Season the duck breasts with salt and pepper and cook over moderately high heat until browned on the bottom, about 3 minutes. Turn the duck breasts, reduce the heat to moderate and cook until browned on the bottom

and medium-rare within, 2 to 3 minutes longer. Transfer the duck breasts to warmed plates.

STEP 4 Add the shallots, jalapeño and remaining ½ teaspoon of rosemary to the skillet and cook over moderately low heat until softened, about 4 minutes. Add the reserved duck marinade and simmer over moderately high heat until syrupy, about 3 minutes. Add the kumquats and their syrup and bring to a simmer. Blend in the Dijon mustard and remaining 1 teaspoon of grainy mustard and remove from the heat. Season with salt and pepper. Pour the kumquat sauce over the duck breasts and serve.

Prep Ahead

The candied kumquat slices can be refrigerated for up to 1 week.

Roast Veal with Marjoram

When New York chef Daniel Humm goes home to Switzerland, he prepares rustic, comforting dishes that evoke his childhood. When he's cooking in the northern, more Germanic part of the country, he serves this simple yet impressive veal roast with spaetzle; in the southern, Italian-leaning region, he makes a luscious risotto with porcini mushrooms. Either way, it's a winner.

TIME	MAKES	CONTRIBUTED BY
15 min active; 1 hr 15 min total	**4 servings**	**Daniel Humm**

One 2½-lb. bone-in veal loin roast, bones frenched

Kosher salt and pepper

1 Tbsp. extra-virgin olive oil

3 garlic cloves—2 thickly sliced, 1 minced

4 marjoram sprigs plus 1 Tbsp. chopped marjoram

½ tsp. finely grated lemon zest plus 2 Tbsp. fresh lemon juice

Spaetzle or risotto, for serving

STEP 1 Preheat the oven to 325°. Season the veal all over with salt and pepper. Heat the olive oil in a medium ovenproof skillet. Add the veal and cook over high heat, turning once or twice, until browned all over, about 4 minutes. Add the sliced garlic and marjoram sprigs, transfer the skillet to the oven and roast for about 45 minutes, turning the meat once or twice, until an instant-read thermometer inserted in the center registers 135°. Let the meat rest for 15 minutes.

STEP 2 Meanwhile, in a small bowl, combine the lemon zest and juice with the chopped marjoram and minced garlic. Season with salt and pepper.

STEP 3 Carve the veal roast into ½-inch-thick slices and transfer to plates. Spoon the marjoram-lemon mixture over the veal and serve with spaetzle or risotto.

WINE TIP

Even though this is a centerpiece roast, veal is a lighter meat, so seek out a less intense red wine to drink with it.

Pork Milanese with Dandelion Green Salad

For her super-crispy Milanese, Food Network star Anne Burrell packs panko onto thin pork loin cutlets so they pass the "hang test" and don't fall off during frying. The dish is usually served with a simple arugula salad, but Burrell tops hers with delightfully bitter dandelion greens tossed with bacon and sautéed apples.

TIME **45 min total**	MAKES **4 to 6 servings**	CONTRIBUTED BY **Anne Burrell**

2 large eggs

1 cup all-purpose flour

2 cups panko

Six 3-oz. pork loin cutlets

Kosher salt and pepper

1 tsp. extra-virgin olive oil, plus more for frying

4 bacon slices (4 oz.), cut crosswise ¼ inch thick

2 Granny Smith apples, peeled and cut into ½-inch dice

½ small red onion, cut into thin strips

½ cup apple cider

2½ Tbsp. apple cider vinegar

½ lb. dandelion greens, thick stems discarded, leaves cut crosswise into 1-inch pieces

STEP 1 Preheat the oven to 200°. Line a large baking sheet with paper towels. In a shallow bowl, beat the eggs with 1 tablespoon of water. Put the flour and panko in 2 shallow bowls.

STEP 2 Season the pork cutlets with salt and pepper. Dredge them in the flour, then dip in the egg, letting the excess drip back into the bowl. Dredge the coated pork in the panko, pressing lightly to help it adhere.

STEP 3 In a large skillet, heat ¼ inch of olive oil until shimmering. Add 3 of the cutlets and fry over moderately high heat, turning once, until browned and just cooked through, about 5 minutes; transfer to the prepared baking sheet. Repeat with the remaining cutlets. Transfer the pork to the oven to keep warm.

STEP 4 Wipe out the skillet and heat the 1 teaspoon of olive oil in it. Add the bacon and cook over moderate heat, stirring, until browned and crisp, 3 to 5 minutes. Add the apples and onion and cook over moderately high heat, stirring occasionally, until the apple just starts to soften, about 3 minutes. Add the apple cider and vinegar and cook until the liquid is reduced by half, about 3 minutes.

STEP 5 Scrape the apple mixture into a large bowl. Add the dandelion greens and toss well. Season with salt and pepper and toss again. Transfer the pork Milanese to plates, top with the salad and serve right away.

Flank Steaks with Shallot–Red Wine Sauce

Bordeaux-based blogger Mimi Thorisson is known for her smart takes on classic, rustic French dishes, like this juicy flank steak (*bavette* in France). She prepares it bistro-style: fried in a searing-hot pan with butter. As an accompaniment, she serves a red wine–and–shallot sauce that gets a touch of sweetness from balsamic vinegar.

TIME **30 min total**	MAKES **4 servings**	CONTRIBUTED BY **Mimi Thorisson**

Two 12-oz. flank steaks, about ¾ inch thick

Kosher salt and pepper

5 Tbsp. unsalted butter

1 Tbsp. extra-virgin olive oil

4 large shallots, thinly sliced

¾ cup dry red wine

2 Tbsp. balsamic vinegar

1 tsp. sugar

STEP 1 Season the steaks generously with salt and pepper. In a large cast-iron skillet, melt 2 tablespoons of the butter. Add the steaks and cook over high heat, turning them once, until medium-rare, about 6 minutes total. Transfer the steaks to a carving board and let them rest for about 10 minutes.

STEP 2 Meanwhile, in a medium saucepan, melt 2 tablespoons of the butter in the olive oil. Add the shallots and cook over moderate heat, stirring occasionally, until they are softened and lightly browned, about 8 minutes. Add the red wine, balsamic vinegar and sugar and simmer until reduced by half, 3 to 5 minutes. Remove the saucepan from the heat and whisk in the remaining 1 tablespoon of butter. Season the sauce with salt and pepper.

STEP 3 Slice the steaks across the grain and serve with the shallot–red wine sauce.

SANGIOVESE
& OTHER MEDIUM-BODIED, TANGY REDS

SANGIOVESE Italy is home to some 2,000 different grape varieties, which makes it a little surprising that so many of the country's most famous wines, including Brunello di Montalcino, Chianti and Morellino di Scansano, are made from just one of those: Sangiovese. However, not all Sangioveses are the same. There are actually a number of distinct clones or types of Sangiovese grapes grown throughout Tuscany, all of which produce noticeably different wines.

Broadly speaking, Sangiovese produces medium-bodied wines that have bright acidity and pronounced tannins, with vibrant red-cherry fruit and an underlying earthiness that becomes ever more apparent as the wines age.

Thanks to cheap fiascos wrapped in wicker and even a star turn in the movie *The Silence of the Lambs* (though why anyone would want to drink Chianti with fava beans is puzzling), Chianti's reputation has struggled. But over the past 10 years, the region of Chianti Classico, in particular, has quietly been producing excellent wines, and offering great value as well. (Chianti Classico is a smaller area within the much larger Chianti region.) Winemakers in Chianti Classico have stricter guidelines for aging their wines before release and for the percentage of Sangiovese that must be present in the blend. Chianti Classicos are superb food wines when

young—vibrant reds that are our go-tos for pastas with tomato or meat sauces and slow-roasted pork dishes. Aged examples are exemplary with anything involving wild game or mushrooms.

Brunello di Montalcino, made from a variant known as Sangiovese Grosso, is entirely different. These wines, made in the southern part of Tuscany, are brawny and tightly wound. They can be quite fierce and impenetrable in their youth, but given time the wines reveal savory spice and floral notes that are outstanding with substantial meat dishes, such as leg of lamb.

BARBERA The great secret of Italy's Piedmont region is that while all the world is clamoring for its Nebbiolo-based wines (Barolo, Barbaresco), farmers and winemakers there are happily reaching for something else— fragrant, fruit-forward Barbera. Widely planted throughout Piedmont, Barbera produces wines that are high in acid, with easygoing tannins and minimal oak influence—much more approachable at an earlier age than Nebbiolo. The beauty of Barbera is that it grows well in areas that Nebbiolo doesn't, which means that most winemakers— even top Barolo producers—have plots of Barbera in their vineyards. These wines are considerably less expensive than their Nebbiolo counterparts, even at the high

end. Look for Barbera from the Alba and Asti regions, which are known for reds full of fresh, wild-berry fruit notes and bright acidity. They'll go perfectly with anything from lighter chicken dishes to spaghetti and meatballs.

TEMPRANILLO Tempranillo is Spain's most widely planted red grape, grown everywhere from Ribera del Duero to Valencia. But the place that's come to be synonymous with the variety is Rioja, Spain's oldest winemaking region. Located in the north-central part of the country, Rioja is divided into three distinct areas: Rioja Alta, Rioja Alavesa and Rioja Baja, each of which puts its own stamp on this distinctive grape. Wines from Rioja Alta tend to have higher acidity and more elegance; Alavesa wines are known for their concentration; and Baja, the warmest of the three regions, produces wines that are boldly fruity. (Many wineries blend grapes from a combination of the three.)

Oak-aging is also a big factor in Rioja. More modern producers typically use new oak to give their wines more structure, whereas traditional producers often use older, more neutral barrels. When young, Tempranillo is lively, with tangy red fruit; later, as it matures, the wine picks up some intriguing bass notes suggesting leather and earth. In Spain, Tempranillo is classically paired with jamón, chorizo or grilled lamb dishes.

Lasagna Puttanesca

What do you get when you combine the lusty, robust flavors of southern Italian puttanesca with cheesy eggplant lasagna? This hearty but not heavy pasta dish packed with a ton of flavor from olives, capers and loads of garlic.

TIME	MAKES	CONTRIBUTED BY
45 min active; 2 hr 30 min total	**10 to 12 servings**	**Kay Chun**

5 Tbsp. extra-virgin olive oil, plus more for tossing and greasing

1 lb. dry lasagna noodles

1 medium onion, finely chopped

1 medium eggplant, diced (½ inch)

Kosher salt and pepper

7 anchovy fillets in oil, chopped

7 garlic cloves, finely chopped

1 cup pitted olives, chopped

3 Tbsp. drained capers

Two 28-oz. cans whole peeled tomatoes and juices, crushed

3 cups fresh ricotta cheese

3 large eggs, lightly beaten

1 lb. mozzarella, thinly sliced

STEP 1 Preheat the oven to 450°. Lightly grease a 9-by-13-inch ceramic baking dish with oil.

STEP 2 In a large pot of salted boiling water, cook the lasagna noodles until they just start to soften, 4 to 5 minutes. Drain, transfer to a baking sheet and toss with olive oil.

STEP 3 In a large saucepan, heat 2 tablespoons of the oil. Add the onion and cook over moderate heat until lightly golden, about 5 minutes. Add the eggplant and the remaining 3 tablespoons of oil; season with salt and pepper. Cook, stirring, for 3 minutes. Add the anchovies and garlic and cook for 1 minute. Stir in the olives, capers and crushed tomatoes. Bring to a boil and cook until the puttanesca sauce is thickened, about 10 minutes. Season with salt and pepper.

STEP 4 Meanwhile, in a bowl, stir the ricotta with the eggs and season with salt and pepper.

STEP 5 Spread 1½ cups of the puttanesca sauce in the prepared baking dish. Top with 5 lasagna noodles and spread with half of the ricotta. Top with another layer of noodles and half of the remaining sauce. Arrange another layer of noodles on top and spread with the remaining ricotta. Repeat with a final layer of noodles and the remaining sauce.

STEP 6 Cover the lasagna with foil and bake for 40 minutes. Uncover and bake for 15 minutes. Arrange the mozzarella slices over the top and bake for 15 minutes longer, until most of the liquid has been absorbed. Let the lasagna stand for 15 minutes before serving.

Make Ahead
The baked lasagna can be refrigerated overnight.

Frascatelli Carbonara

New York City chef Michael Romano creates a cream-enriched carbonara sauce that hugs frascatelli, a dense, spaetzle-like pasta that couldn't be easier to make at home. All you do is toss semolina flour with water until small lumps of dough form, then boil until tender.

TIME **45 min total**	MAKES **4 servings**	CONTRIBUTED BY **Michael Romano**

1 Tbsp. extra-virgin olive oil

6 oz. pancetta, sliced ¼ inch thick and cut crosswise into 1-inch-wide strips

1 cup heavy cream

Black pepper

½ cup freshly grated Parmesan cheese

½ cup freshly grated pecorino cheese, plus more for serving

1 large egg yolk

2 Tbsp. kosher salt

1 lb. semolina flour (2½ cups)

STEP 1 In a large skillet, heat the oil. Add the pancetta and cook over moderate heat until crisp, about 7 minutes. Drain the pancetta in a strainer over a bowl; reserve 2 tablespoons of the fat.

STEP 2 Add the cream to the skillet and bring to a simmer over moderate heat. Grind black pepper into the cream, then add the Parmesan and the ½ cup of pecorino, stirring until blended, about 2 minutes. Scrape the mixture into a medium bowl and let cool. Whisk in the egg yolk, pancetta and the reserved pancetta fat; refrigerate the sauce.

STEP 3 Bring 4 quarts of water to a boil; add the salt. Spread the semolina on a large rimmed baking sheet. Put 1 cup of cold water in a bowl. Dip your fingertips in the water and scatter drops all over the surface of the semolina. Keep scattering water until the entire surface is covered with drops. With a rubber spatula, turn the moistened semolina over on itself, tossing to form small lumps. Shake the sheet to spread the loose semolina in an even layer. Repeat with more water until just about all of the semolina

has been formed into irregular lumps about the size of small peas. Shake the frascatelli in a colander to remove any loose semolina.

STEP 4 Pour the frascatelli into the boiling water and cook, stirring a few times, until al dente, about 4 minutes.

STEP 5 Meanwhile, in a large, deep skillet, gently reheat the sauce over moderately low heat, stirring constantly. Drain the frascatelli, add it to the sauce and bring to a simmer, stirring. Transfer the frascatelli to shallow bowls and serve, passing grated pecorino at the table.

Make Ahead
The cream sauce can be refrigerated overnight.

Pasta Bolognese

Who says you have to devote an entire afternoon to making Bolognese sauce? This traditionally long-simmered ragù tastes just as good when cooked for less than half an hour. The trick: Stock and tomato paste add an almost-instant savory depth.

TIME **45 min total**	MAKES **4 servings**	CONTRIBUTED BY **F&W Test Kitchen**

2 Tbsp. unsalted butter

¼ lb. sliced bacon, cut crosswise into ¼-inch-wide strips

1 onion, chopped

½ lb. ground beef or a mixture of pork, veal and beef

1 cup beef or chicken stock or low-sodium broth

½ cup dry white wine

2 Tbsp. tomato paste

½ tsp. dried oregano

¾ tsp. salt

¼ tsp. black pepper

½ cup heavy cream

¾ lb. spaghetti

2 Tbsp. chopped parsley

STEP 1 In a large skillet, heat the butter and bacon over moderately low heat. Cook until the bacon renders some of its fat, about 3 minutes. Add the chopped onion and cook, stirring occasionally, until starting to soften, about 3 minutes. Stir in the ground beef and cook until the meat is no longer pink, about 2 minutes. Add the stock, wine, tomato paste, oregano, salt and pepper. Simmer, stirring occasionally, until the sauce thickens, about 25 minutes. Stir in the cream and remove from the heat.

STEP 2 In a large pot of salted boiling water, cook the spaghetti until just done, about 12 minutes. Drain, toss with the sauce and the parsley and serve.

WINE TIP It's hard to imagine a more classic pairing for this rich Bolognese than a savory Chianti Classico.

Beef Tallarín Saltado

This pasta from Ricardo Zarate of Rosaliné in L.A. is a riff on *tallarín saltado,* a comfort food in the chef's native Lima that's like a Chinese-Peruvian chow mein. Zarate makes his version almost Bolognese-style, with ground beef, tomatoes and tagliatelle, but key to the dish is the *lomo saltado* sauce, a garlicky puree of red wine vinegar, chile paste and soy.

TIME	MAKES	CONTRIBUTED BY
35 min total	**4 servings**	**Ricardo Zarate**

7 garlic cloves, chopped

One 1-inch piece of fresh ginger, peeled and chopped

3 Tbsp. red wine vinegar

1 Tbsp. ají amarillo paste (see Note)

¼ tsp. freshly ground black pepper

3 Tbsp. soy sauce

1 lb. dried tagliatelle

2 Tbsp. canola oil

¾ lb. ground beef sirloin (90% lean)

1 medium red onion, finely diced

2 plum tomatoes—halved, seeded and finely diced

1 cup chicken stock or low-sodium broth

½ cup freshly grated Parmesan cheese, plus shavings for garnish

2 Tbsp. minced cilantro

Kosher salt

STEP 1 In a blender or mini food processor, combine the garlic, ginger, vinegar, ají amarillo paste, black pepper and 1 tablespoon of the soy sauce; puree until smooth. Reserve the *lomo saltado* sauce.

STEP 2 In a large pot of salted boiling water, cook the pasta until al dente. Drain well.

STEP 3 Meanwhile, in a large skillet, heat the oil. Add the ground beef and cook over high heat, stirring to break up the meat, until browned, 3 to 4 minutes. Using a slotted spoon, transfer the meat to a bowl.

STEP 4 Add the onion to the skillet and cook over moderate heat, stirring occasionally, until softened, about 5 minutes. Add the meat and tomatoes and cook over high heat for 1 minute, then add the remaining 2 tablespoons of soy sauce and boil for 1 minute. Stir in the chicken stock and *lomo saltado* sauce and bring to a boil.

STEP 5 Add the pasta and grated Parmesan to the sauce and toss to coat. Fold in the cilantro and season with salt. Transfer to a bowl, garnish with Parmesan shavings and serve.

Note

Ají amarillo paste, a spicy Peruvian yellow chile paste, is available at many supermarkets and online from amazon.com.

Pasta with Guanciale, Radicchio & Ricotta

To make this rich dish, L.A. chef Nancy Silverton sautés *guanciale* (cured pork jowl) and then cooks the radicchio and red onions in the rendered fat. She likes to use a pasta called calamarata—which looks like thick squid rings—to catch the sauce, but any wide, tubular shape works great here.

TIME	MAKES	CONTRIBUTED BY
30 min total	**6 servings**	**Nancy Silverton**

½ lb. calamarata or other short, wide, tubular pasta

¼ cup extra-virgin olive oil, plus more for drizzling

3 medium red onions, cut into 8 wedges each

Kosher salt and pepper

6 oz. *guanciale* or pancetta, cut into ¼-inch dice

¾ cup freshly grated Pecorino Romano cheese

¼ small head of radicchio, torn into 2-inch pieces

⅓ cup fresh ricotta cheese

¼ cup chopped walnuts

STEP 1 In a large pot of salted boiling water, cook the pasta until al dente, about 8 minutes. Drain the pasta, reserving ½ cup of the cooking water.

STEP 2 Meanwhile, in a large, straight-sided skillet, heat the ¼ cup of olive oil. Add the onions, season with salt and toss to coat with the oil. Cook over high heat until the onions are just beginning to soften, about 1 minute. Stir in ¾ cup of water and cook until the water is evaporated and the onions are just tender, about 6 minutes. Stir in the *guanciale* and cook, stirring, until the fat is rendered and the *guanciale* is lightly browned and crisp, about 7 minutes.

STEP 3 Carefully drain off all but 2 tablespoons of the fat from the skillet. Stir in the pasta along with the pecorino, radicchio and the reserved pasta water. Cook over high heat, stirring constantly, until hot, about 1 minute. Season the pasta with salt and pepper and top with dollops of the ricotta. Transfer the pasta to a large serving dish, sprinkle with the walnuts and drizzle with olive oil. Serve immediately.

Preserved-Tomato Paccheri

For her unconventional tomato sauce, Missy Robbins, chef at Brooklyn's Lilia, deploys her preserving skills to marinate tomatoes in a mix of garlic, spices, citrus and warm olive oil. The result is a supple, fresh and incredibly flavorful coating for tubular paccheri pasta. To pair with the dish, Robbins loves the high-toned aromatics of La Miraja's Le Masche Barbera d'Asti.

TIME	MAKES	CONTRIBUTED BY
1 hr active; 6 hr total	**6 servings**	**Missy Robbins**

Four 28-oz. cans whole San Marzano tomatoes—drained, halved lengthwise and seeded

4½ tsp. sugar

Kosher salt

1 Tbsp. fennel seeds

1 Tbsp. coriander seeds

2 cups plus 3 Tbsp. extra-virgin olive oil

7 garlic cloves—2 crushed, 5 thinly sliced

Wide strips of zest from 2 small lemons plus 1 tsp. finely grated zest

Wide strips of zest from 1 small orange

2 basil sprigs

2 marjoram sprigs plus 2 tsp. marjoram leaves

1½ tsp. crushed red pepper

1 lb. paccheri or other wide, tubular pasta

¼ cup freshly grated Pecorino Romano cheese, for garnish

STEP 1 Put the tomato halves in a colander set over a bowl. Sprinkle with the sugar and 4½ teaspoons of kosher salt and toss gently. Let stand at room temperature for 2 hours.

STEP 2 Meanwhile, in a small skillet, toast the fennel and coriander seeds over moderately low heat, shaking the pan, until very fragrant, about 2 minutes. Transfer the seeds to a spice grinder or mortar and let cool slightly, then coarsely grind.

STEP 3 In a small saucepan, combine 2 cups of the olive oil, the crushed seeds, crushed garlic, lemon and orange zest strips and the basil and marjoram sprigs. Warm over low heat until the oil begins to bubble, about 7 minutes. Transfer the drained tomatoes to a deep ceramic baking dish and pour the warm oil over them. Let stand at room temperature for 3 hours.

STEP 4 Using a slotted spoon, transfer the preserved tomatoes to a bowl. Using your hands or a metal spoon, coarsely crush them; you should have 3 cups.

STEP 5 In a large skillet, warm the remaining 3 tablespoons of olive oil over moderate heat. Add the sliced garlic and cook, stirring, until fragrant but not browned, about 2 minutes. Add the crushed tomatoes and crushed red pepper and cook until the tomatoes are warmed through, about 2 minutes; keep warm over low heat.

STEP 6 In a pot of salted boiling water, cook the paccheri until al dente. Drain well. Add to the skillet and stir to coat. Stir in the grated lemon zest and the marjoram leaves. Transfer the paccheri to a bowl, garnish with the cheese and serve.

Shellfish–Tomato Stew on Soft–Cooked Polenta

WINE **TIP**

Shellfish and oak don't go very well together, so stick to younger reds like a basic Chianti rather than a longer-aged riserva here.

At the Casa Olivi villa in Treia, Italy, owner Sophie Heaulme loves to take advantage of the bounty from the nearby Adriatic. Here, she makes a tomato stew with shrimp, squid and mussels over creamy polenta.

TIME **45 min total**	MAKES **6 servings**	CONTRIBUTED BY **Sophie Heaulme**

1 Tbsp. extra-virgin olive oil

1 small onion, diced

6 garlic cloves, minced

One 28-oz. can diced tomatoes

¾ cup dry white wine

Kosher salt and pepper

1½ cups chicken stock or low-sodium broth

1 cup milk

1 cup instant polenta

3 Tbsp. unsalted butter

1 lb. large shrimp, shelled and deveined

1 lb. cleaned small squid—bodies cut crosswise into ½-inch rings, tentacles left whole

2 lbs. mussels, scrubbed

2 Tbsp. chopped parsley

STEP 1 In a large pot, heat the oil. Add the onion and cook over moderately low heat until softened, about 5 minutes. Add the garlic and cook, stirring, until fragrant, about 2 minutes. Add the tomatoes and bring to a simmer. Stir in the wine and cook over moderate heat for 2 minutes. Season with salt and pepper; set aside.

STEP 2 In a medium saucepan, bring the stock, milk and 2 cups of water to a boil. Gradually whisk in the polenta. Cook over moderate heat, whisking, until the polenta is slightly thickened, about 2 minutes. Stir in 2 tablespoons of the butter and season with salt and pepper. Cover and keep warm.

STEP 3 Bring the tomato sauce back to a simmer. Add the shrimp and squid and simmer over moderately high heat until barely cooked, about 2 minutes. Add the mussels, cover and cook until they open, about 4 minutes. Discard any mussels that do not open. Swirl in the remaining 1 tablespoon of butter and the parsley. Season with salt and pepper.

STEP 4 Whisk the polenta and ladle it into bowls. Spoon the stew over the polenta and serve.

Pork Shank Osso Buco

In place of the veal shanks typically used in osso buco, Jimmy Bannos, Jr., of The Purple Pig in Chicago braises pork shanks with tomatoes and wine. He adds anchovies, crushed red pepper and lemon zest to the braise, creating a complex and deeply flavored sauce that's so satisfying spooned over soft polenta.

TIME **1 hr active; 4 hr total, plus overnight salting**	MAKES **6 to 8 servings**	CONTRIBUTED BY **Jimmy Bannos, Jr.**

6 pork shanks (7½ lbs.; see Note)

Kosher salt and black pepper

3 Tbsp. extra-virgin olive oil

1 large white onion, chopped

1 large carrot, chopped

1 celery rib, chopped

3 garlic cloves, minced

2 anchovy fillets, minced

1 Tbsp. finely grated lemon zest

½ tsp. crushed red pepper

1 cup dry white wine

Two 28-oz. cans crushed tomatoes

2 cups chicken stock or low-sodium broth

5 thyme sprigs

2 rosemary sprigs

2 bay leaves

Creamy polenta, for serving

STEP 1 In a baking dish, season the pork shanks with salt and black pepper. Cover and refrigerate overnight.

STEP 2 Preheat the oven to 325°. In a large enameled cast-iron casserole, heat the olive oil until shimmering. Add 3 of the shanks in a single layer and cook over moderately high heat, turning occasionally, until browned, about 8 minutes. Transfer the shanks to a large roasting pan. Repeat with the remaining 3 shanks.

STEP 3 Pour off all but 2 tablespoons of the fat from the casserole. Add the onion, carrot, celery and a generous pinch each of salt and black pepper and cook over moderately high heat, stirring occasionally, until the vegetables are softened and just starting to brown, about 10 minutes. Stir in the garlic, anchovies, lemon zest and crushed red pepper and cook until fragrant. Add the wine and simmer until reduced by half, about 3 minutes. Add the

tomatoes, stock, thyme, rosemary and bay leaves and bring to a boil. Pour the mixture over the shanks in the roasting pan. Cover tightly with foil and braise in the oven for about 3 hours, until the meat is very tender.

STEP 4 Transfer the pork shanks to a platter and tent with foil. Discard the herbs and spoon off the fat from the sauce. Working in batches, puree the sauce in a blender until smooth. Season with salt and black pepper. Spoon some of the sauce over the pork shanks and pass the remaining sauce at the table. Serve the osso buco with creamy polenta.

Note
Pork shanks are available at some supermarkets and online from dartagnan.com.

Make Ahead
The pork shanks can be refrigerated in the sauce for up to 2 days. Reheat gently.

Baked Polenta Casserole

This take on Roman-style gnocchi—polenta and cheese baked under a blanket of tomato sauce—is much quicker to make than the more familiar but labor-intensive dumplings.

TIME	MAKES	CONTRIBUTED BY
10 min active; 35 min total	**8 servings**	**Jonathon Sawyer**

4 cups whole milk

2 cups instant polenta

2 cups freshly grated Pecorino Romano cheese

4 Tbsp. unsalted butter

Pinch of freshly grated nutmeg

Kosher salt and pepper

2 large eggs, lightly beaten

2 cups tomato sauce

Preheat the oven to 350°. In a large saucepan, bring the milk and 3 cups of water to a boil. Slowly whisk in the polenta. Cook over low heat, whisking constantly, until thick, about 3 minutes. Whisk in 1½ cups of the pecorino, the butter and the nutmeg; season with salt and pepper. Whisk in the eggs in a slow, steady stream; transfer to a 9-by-13-inch baking dish. Spread the tomato sauce over the polenta and sprinkle with the remaining ½ cup of pecorino. Bake until the cheese is melted and the sauce is bubbling, about 20 minutes. Let rest for 5 minutes before serving.

Chicken Scarpariello

For a shortcut version of scarpariello—chicken sautéed in a tangy lemon sauce with bell peppers—use fast-cooking boneless thighs and jarred Peppadew peppers .

TIME	MAKES	CONTRIBUTED BY
40 min total	**4 servings**	**Grace Parisi**

8 small skinless, boneless chicken thighs (2 lbs.)

Kosher salt and pepper

All-purpose flour, for dusting

½ cup extra-virgin olive oil

8 garlic cloves, halved lengthwise and lightly smashed

4 large rosemary sprigs, broken into 2-inch pieces

2 cups chicken stock

2 Tbsp. fresh lemon juice

2 Tbsp. unsalted butter

½ cup Peppadew peppers, sliced

STEP 1 Season the chicken with salt and pepper; dust with flour. In a large skillet, heat the oil until shimmering. Cook the chicken over high heat, turning once, until browned and crusty, 10 minutes. Add the garlic and rosemary; cook for 3 minutes, until the garlic is lightly browned. Transfer the chicken to a platter; leave the rosemary and garlic in the skillet.

STEP 2 Add the stock to the skillet; cook over high heat, scraping up any browned bits, until reduced by half, 5 minutes. Add the lemon juice and butter and swirl until emulsified. Return the chicken and any juices to the skillet. Add the peppers and cook, turning the chicken to coat in the sauce, about 3 minutes. Transfer the chicken and sauce to the platter and serve.

Roast Chicken with Sausage & Peppers

F&W's Justin Chapple combines all the flavors of an Italian sausage sub in this fun and delicious dish. He roasts a chicken on top of a Bundt pan, exposing the whole bird to even heat, as with a rotisserie. As a bonus, the drippings flavor the sausages and vegetables in the bottom of the pan.

TIME	MAKES	CONTRIBUTED BY
30 min active; 1 hr 45 min total	**4 servings**	**Justin Chapple**

¾ lb. hot Italian sausages, halved crosswise

3 Italian frying peppers or Cubanelles, halved lengthwise and seeded

2 large red bell peppers, cut into large strips

2 large red onions, cut into 1-inch wedges

2 Tbsp. extra-virgin olive oil, plus more for brushing

2 Tbsp. dried oregano

Kosher salt and pepper

One 4-lb. whole chicken

2 tsp. grated lemon zest

STEP 1 Preheat the oven to 450°. Wrap the center pillar of a 10-inch Bundt pan with foil.

STEP 2 In a large bowl, toss the sausages with all of the peppers, the onions, the 2 tablespoons of olive oil and 1 tablespoon of the oregano. Season with salt and pepper and add to the pan.

STEP 3 Brush the chicken with olive oil and season with salt, pepper, the remaining 1 tablespoon of oregano and the lemon zest. Perch the chicken on the pan by inserting the center pillar into the cavity.

STEP 4 Roast the chicken for about 1 hour, until an instant-read thermometer inserted in the inner thighs registers 155°. Transfer to a board; let rest for 15 minutes.

STEP 5 Transfer the sausages, peppers, onions and pan juices to a platter. Carve the chicken and arrange on the platter. Serve.

Serve With
Crusty bread.

WINE TIP

For hot sausages, choose a medium-bodied red. Bigger, more tannic wines can make the spices turn harsh.

Glazed Agrodolce Ribs

These tender, juicy ribs are flavored with Tuscan seasonings—garlic, fennel seeds and fresh herbs—and quickly glazed under the broiler with a balsamic-laced barbecue sauce. You can also brush the sauce on burgers, portobellos and sweet potato wedges on the grill for a sweet-tangy burnished sheen.

TIME	MAKES	CONTRIBUTED BY
45 min active; 2 hr 45 min total	**8 servings**	**Justin Chapple**

Two 4-lb. racks of pork spareribs, membranes removed

1½ Tbsp. fennel seeds, crushed

1½ Tbsp. finely chopped thyme

2 tsp. crushed red pepper

2 tsp. finely chopped rosemary

Kosher salt and black pepper

2 Tbsp. extra-virgin olive oil

1 small red onion, coarsely grated

3 garlic cloves, finely grated

1 cup balsamic vinegar

¼ cup white distilled vinegar

1 cup ketchup

¾ cup packed light brown sugar

STEP 1 Preheat the oven to 325°. Line 2 large rimmed baking sheets with foil and set the ribs on them, meaty side up. In a mortar, crush the fennel seeds with the thyme, crushed red pepper, rosemary, 1½ tablespoons of salt and 2 teaspoons of black pepper. Rub the spice mix all over the ribs and roast for about 2 hours, until the meat is tender.

STEP 2 Meanwhile, in a medium saucepan, heat the olive oil. Add the onion, garlic and a generous pinch of salt and cook over moderately high heat, stirring, until the onion is softened, 3 to 5 minutes. Add both vinegars along with the ketchup and brown sugar and bring to a boil. Simmer over moderate heat, stirring frequently, until the sauce is thick and reduced to 2 cups, about 15 minutes.

STEP 3 Remove the ribs from the oven and turn on the broiler. Brush the underside of the racks with some of the sauce. Broil 1 sheet of ribs 8 inches from the heat until browned. Flip the ribs and repeat on the other side. Move the ribs to the bottom rack of the oven to keep warm while you glaze the rest.

STEP 4 Transfer the racks to a work surface. Cut in between the bones to form individual ribs and mound on a platter. Pass the remaining sauce at the table.

Prep Ahead
The sauce can be refrigerated for up to 1 week.

Dry-Aged Roast Beef with Fresh Hot Sauce

"I love this dish," says Stuart Brioza of State Bird Provisions in San Francisco. "It's a pretty traditional roast beef, almost like an Italian *tagliata* [sliced steak], but then you shake it up by serving it with crispy garlic chips and a fresh-chile hot sauce." The beef is salt-cured, so it's extra juicy; served on a bed of arugula, with the bright red hot sauce, it couldn't be more festive.

TIME **30 min active; 1 hr 45 min total, plus 1 day curing**	MAKES **6 to 8 servings**	CONTRIBUTED BY **Stuart Brioza**

ROAST BEEF

One 4-lb. dry-aged sirloin roast

2 tsp. kosher salt

1 tsp. freshly ground pepper

HOT SAUCE

½ lb. red Fresno or red jalapeño chiles—stemmed, seeded and coarsely chopped

1 garlic clove, crushed

½ cup fresh lime juice

¼ cup water

2 Tbsp. kosher salt

GARNISHES

½ cup whole milk

½ cup very thinly sliced garlic (sliced on a mandoline)

Canola oil, for frying

Kosher salt and pepper

2 cups baby arugula

Extra-virgin olive oil, for drizzling

2 scallions, thinly sliced

STEP 1 PREPARE THE ROAST BEEF Set the roast on a baking sheet and rub it all over with the salt and pepper. Refrigerate, uncovered, for 1 day.

STEP 2 Preheat the oven to 400°. Heat a large cast-iron skillet. Cook the roast, fat side down, over moderately high heat until well browned, about 3 minutes. Continue cooking, turning, until the meat is browned all over, about 5 minutes. Turn the meat fat side up, transfer to the oven and roast for 40 to 45 minutes, until an instant-read thermometer inserted in the center registers 125° for medium-rare. Transfer the roast to a cutting board and let rest for 15 minutes.

STEP 3 MEANWHILE, MAKE THE HOT SAUCE In a blender, combine all of the ingredients and puree until smooth. Strain into a medium bowl.

STEP 4 MAKE THE GARNISHES In a small saucepan, bring the milk and garlic just to a boil. Drain the garlic and pat the slices dry on paper towels. In a small saucepan, heat ½ inch of canola oil to 275°. Working in 2 batches, fry the garlic, stirring, until light golden, 1 to 2 minutes. Using a slotted spoon, transfer the garlic to paper towels to drain. Season with salt and let cool.

STEP 5 Spread the arugula on a platter. Thinly slice the roast and arrange on the arugula. Drizzle a little hot sauce and olive oil over the meat and garnish with the garlic chips and scallions. Season with salt and pepper and serve the remaining hot sauce at the table.

Prep Ahead

The hot sauce can be refrigerated for 1 week. The garlic chips can be stored for 1 day in an airtight container.

Sausage & Potato Pan Roast

This one-pan dish is the perfect cold-weather weeknight dinner. Simply roast sausages with potatoes and shallots and toss them with lemony arugula before serving.

TIME **20 min active; 55 min total**	MAKES **4 to 6 servings**	CONTRIBUTED BY **Justin Chapple**

2 large red potatoes, cut into 1½-inch pieces

2 Yukon Gold potatoes, cut into 1-inch wedges

1 large baking potato, cut into 1½-inch pieces

10 medium unpeeled shallots, halved

⅓ cup extra-virgin olive oil, plus more for brushing

Kosher salt and pepper

1½ lbs. sweet Italian sausage, cut into 3-inch lengths

One 8-oz. bunch of arugula, stemmed and chopped

1 Tbsp. fresh lemon juice

STEP 1 Preheat the oven to 425°. On a large rimmed baking sheet, toss all of the potatoes with the shallots and the ⅓ cup of oil. Season generously with salt and pepper. Roast for about

15 minutes, until the potatoes are lightly browned. Brush the sausage with oil and add to the baking sheet. Roast for 20 to 25 minutes longer, until the potatoes are tender and the sausage is cooked through.

STEP 2 Transfer everything on the sheet to a platter. Fold in the arugula and lemon juice, season with salt and pepper and serve.

Roasted Veal Chops with Grapes

New York Times food columnist Melissa Clark roasts juicy red grapes alongside tender veal chops, cooking the fruit down to an intensely jammy condiment.

TIME **25 min total**	MAKES **4 servings**	CONTRIBUTED BY **Melissa Clark**

1 lb. seedless red grapes

3 Tbsp. sherry vinegar

2½ Tbsp. unsalted butter, softened

½ tsp. sugar

Kosher salt and pepper

Four 1-inch-thick veal rib chops (about ½ lb. each)

STEP 1 Preheat the oven to 500°. On a sturdy rimmed baking sheet, toss the grapes with the vinegar, 1½ tablespoons of the butter and the sugar; season with salt and pepper. Roast for about 10 minutes, shaking the baking sheet halfway through, until the grapes are hot and the pan is sizzling.

STEP 2 Rub the chops with the remaining butter; season with salt and pepper. Push the grapes to one side. Add the chops and roast for 5 minutes, until sizzling underneath. Turn the chops and roast for 5 minutes for medium-rare. Transfer to a platter, scrape the grapes on top and serve.

Lamb Steak Frites

Whole and butterflied legs of lamb are familiar cuts, but steaks cut from the leg are much less common. They're worth trying, especially because they're easy to prepare and cook so quickly. Here, Boston chef Tony Maws pan-roasts the steaks, basting them with a flavorful herb-infused butter, then serves them with fries as a clever variation on classic steak frites.

TIME **30 min total**	MAKES **4 servings**	CONTRIBUTED BY **Tony Maws**

Two 1¼-lb. lamb leg steaks, cut about 1¼ inches thick

½ tsp. ground cumin

½ tsp. ground fennel seeds

Kosher salt and pepper

2 Tbsp. canola oil

4 small thyme sprigs

2 garlic cloves

6 Tbsp. unsalted butter, cubed

1 shallot, minced

1 cup dry red wine

1 cup chicken stock or low-sodium broth

French fries, for serving

STEP 1 Rub the lamb with the cumin and fennel; season with salt and pepper. In a cast-iron skillet, heat the oil until smoking. Add the lamb and cook over high heat, turning once, until browned. Reduce the heat to moderate. Add the thyme, garlic and 4 tablespoons of the butter and cook for 5 minutes, basting the lamb with the butter. Turn the steaks and cook, basting, until an instant-read thermometer inserted in the thickest part registers 130°, about 5 minutes; transfer to a carving board and let rest for 10 minutes. Thickly slice against the grain.

STEP 2 Pour off all but 1 tablespoon of the fat from the skillet. Add the shallot and cook over moderately high heat until softened, 1 minute. Add the wine and simmer until syrupy, 4 minutes. Add the chicken stock and simmer until slightly reduced, 3 minutes. Off the heat, whisk in the remaining 2 tablespoons of butter; season with salt and pepper. Serve with the lamb and french fries.

WINE TIP

One good tip for cooking with wine: At the very least, use a wine you'd also be willing to drink.

SYRAH
& OTHER SPICY, FULL-BODIED REDS

SYRAH If there's one word to describe Syrah, it's "intense." Great Syrahs are inky and brooding, evoking dark fruit and freshly cracked black pepper and bacon all at once. Syrah loves sun and warmth, which explains its affinity for regions like France's Rhône, Australia's Barossa and Washington state's Walla Walla. But cool nighttime temperatures are equally important, helping to preserve the grape's aromatics and acidity and keeping Syrah from being just a wallop of richness.

France is Syrah's native home, with the most famous (and pricey) versions coming from the northern Rhône hillsides of Côte-Rôtie, Cornas and Hermitage. Farther south, in the Côtes du Rhône, Syrah is most often blended with other varieties, like Grenache, producing wines that are better for drinking earlier, with less overt tannin and more generous fruit.

Australia has worked to harness Syrah's fruity side since the 1800s (it's called Shiraz there). For a long time the Aussie Shiraz style was very ripe, with high alcohol and sweet blackberry flavors; most big wineries paid less attention to the grape's nuances than to its ripe fruitiness. Now, many producers in regions like Barossa and McLaren Vale are shifting toward a more subtle style. The story is similar in South Africa's Stellenbosch, where Shiraz has been planted in cooler areas, with great results.

In the US, California's Central Coast has been a source for Syrah since the 1970s. Areas like Santa Barbara and Santa Maria Valley also produce fruit-forward styles, though less so than Australian versions. In southeastern Washington, Walla Walla is one of the best places for Syrah in the States. This desert-like region has sunny days that recall the hills of the Rhône and a similar cool-down at night: a recipe for inky, bold, intense wines.

Very little goes as well with Syrah as lamb, but any substantial meat dish will find a friend here: Burgers, pulled pork, rib roasts and barbecue are all great possibilities.

GRENACHE This grape has an undeniably friendly disposition. At their best, wines made from Grenache explode with red-berry fruit, moderated by a peppery edge and fine tannins. Thanks to its compelling personality, Grenache is grown around the world. In France its home is in the Rhône Valley, where it plays the leading role in Châteauneuf-du-Pape blends and simpler Côtes du Rhône reds, but it's grown throughout the south of the country. It's also widely planted in Spain, where it's known as Garnacha. Full-bodied Priorat reds are often mostly Grenache, and the variety is also found in Navarra and Aragón, where it produces lively everyday wines. In Australia, Grenache is popular in GSM (Grenache, Shiraz,

Mourvèdre) bottlings, rounding out the edges of its more aggressive partners. In the US, an emerging crew of Central Coast winemakers focuses on Grenache's lighthearted fruitiness, harvesting earlier than usual to pull back the variety's tendency toward high alcohol and jamminess. More serious versions of Grenache are ideal with roasts and stews, whereas easygoing, medium-bodied styles are great picnic wines or partners for cheesy pastas or simple roast chicken.

MALBEC Despite the fact that Malbec originated in France and plays a supporting role in many Bordeaux (and Bordeaux-inspired) blends, Argentina's Mendoza region is where the grape has achieved its greatest renown. Malbec is beloved for its undeniably purple flavors—juicy dark berries and plums, violets and lilacs—and its exuberantly spicy aromatics. All this opulence can easily add up to an overripe, pruney wine in the wrong hands, but over the past decade, vintners in Mendoza have gotten better at isolating the most promising vineyard areas and methods for working with the grape. Argentina's best Malbecs come from high-altitude vineyards at the base of the Andes, where the cooler, dry climate gives the wines necessary freshness and acidity. Cliché though it may seem, Malbec pairs fantastically with grilled meats: big steaks, racks of lamb and double-thick pork chops, for instance.

Chicken with Port & Figs

Dried figs are poached in port to make a luscious sauce for this juicy chicken. Ruby port provides a rich, beautiful color, but tawny will also taste great. To get that gorgeous golden-brown exterior, start the bird in the oven, and when the meat is almost done, crank up the broiler to crisp the skin all over.

TIME	MAKES	CONTRIBUTED BY
50 min total	**4 servings**	**F&W Test Kitchen**

8 dried figs, tough stems removed

⅔ cup plus 1 Tbsp. port

Two 3-inch-long strips of lemon zest

One 3- to 3½-lb. chicken, quartered

1 Tbsp. extra-virgin olive oil

Kosher salt and pepper

1 Tbsp. butter, cut into 4 pieces

STEP 1 Preheat the oven to 375°. Pierce each fig three or four times with a paring knife. In a small stainless steel saucepan, combine the figs with 1 cup of water, the ⅔ cup of port and the lemon zest. Bring to a boil and simmer, covered, until the figs are tender, about 30 minutes. Discard the zest and reserve the poaching liquid. Cut the figs in half.

STEP 2 Meanwhile, coat the chicken with the oil and arrange the pieces skin side up in a large roasting pan. Sprinkle the chicken with the remaining 1 tablespoon of port and season with ¼ teaspoon of salt and ⅛ teaspoon of pepper. Top each piece of chicken with a piece of the butter. Transfer the pan to the oven and cook until the breasts are just done, about 30 minutes. Remove the breasts and continue to cook the legs until done, about 5 minutes longer. Remove the roasting pan from the oven; return the breasts to the pan.

STEP 3 Heat the broiler. Broil the chicken until the skin is golden brown, about 2 minutes. Transfer the chicken to a plate.

STEP 4 Pour off the fat from the roasting pan. Set the pan over moderate heat and add the fig-poaching liquid. Bring to a boil, scraping up any brown bits from the bottom. Boil until the liquid is reduced to approximately ¼ cup, 4 minutes. Add the figs, any accumulated juices from the chicken and a pinch each of salt and pepper. Spoon the sauce over the chicken.

Serve With

A green vegetable, such as steamed broccoli, makes a quick and easy side dish.

Chicken Drumsticks with Asian Barbecue Sauce

With all due respect for traditional American-style barbecue sauce, we love this sweet, sticky, slightly fiery version using Asian ingredients, including chile sauce, hoisin, rice vinegar and ginger.

TIME	MAKES	CONTRIBUTED BY
20 min active; 1 hr total	**8 servings**	**Grace Parisi**

2 Tbsp. vegetable oil

1 tsp. Chinese five-spice powder

16 chicken drumsticks (3 lbs.)

Kosher salt and pepper

¾ cup hoisin sauce

¼ cup sweet Asian chile sauce or hot pepper jelly

¼ cup unseasoned rice vinegar

¼ cup chicken stock or low-sodium broth

2 Tbsp. minced peeled fresh ginger

2 large garlic cloves

1 tsp. toasted sesame oil

1 cup toasted sesame seeds

STEP 1 Preheat the oven to 425°. In a large bowl, mix the vegetable oil with the five-spice powder. Add the chicken, season with salt and pepper and toss. Arrange the drumsticks on a foil-lined baking sheet. Roast for about 35 minutes, turning twice, until cooked.

STEP 2 Meanwhile, in a blender, combine the hoisin sauce, chile sauce, rice vinegar, stock, ginger, garlic and sesame oil and puree until very smooth. Transfer to a saucepan and simmer until slightly thickened, 5 minutes.

STEP 3 Transfer the chicken to a bowl and toss with the sauce until completely coated.

STEP 4 Preheat the broiler and position a rack 8 inches from the heat. Return the chicken to the baking sheet and broil for about 10 minutes, brushing with the sauce and turning occasionally, until glazed and sticky.

STEP 5 Add the sesame seeds to a bowl. Dip the chicken in the seeds to coat, then serve.

Slow-Cooker Apple Cider Pulled Pork

It's no secret that apples and pork go great together. Here, instead of cooking with fresh fruit, pork butt is simmered slowly in cider. The result is pull-apart-tender meat infused with tangy-sweet apple flavor.

TIME	MAKES	CONTRIBUTED BY
30 min active; 7 hr 30 min total	**6 to 8 servings**	**Ian Knauer**

One 7- to 8-lb. bone-in pork butt

6 garlic cloves, thinly sliced

Kosher salt and pepper

2 Tbsp. vegetable oil

1 medium onion, sliced

4 cups apple cider

Rolls, for serving

STEP 1 Score the pork skin in a crosshatch pattern with a sharp knife. Using a paring knife, make 1-inch-deep incisions all over the pork and insert 1 slice of garlic in each one. Season the meat with 1½ teaspoons of salt and ¾ teaspoon of pepper.

STEP 2 In a 5- to 6-quart slow cooker, heat the oil on high until hot. Add the pork butt and cook, turning once, until browned, 6 to 8 minutes. Transfer the pork to a plate. Stir the onion into the slow cooker and cook, scraping up any browned bits, until golden, about 6 minutes. Return the pork butt to the slow cooker along with the cider. Cover the slow cooker and simmer on low until the meat is very tender, 7 to 8 hours.

STEP 3 Transfer the pork to a bowl and shred with 2 forks, discarding the bone. Return the meat to the cooking liquid and season with salt and pepper. Serve with rolls.

WINE TIP Spicy, robust Syrahs are made to go with rich BBQ-style dishes like this one.

Classic Blue Cheese Burgers

Based on the custom beef blend that April Bloomfield is famous for at her NYC gastropub, The Spotted Pig, these juicy burgers are simply topped with melted blue cheese—that's all the adornment the flavorful patties need.

TIME	MAKES	CONTRIBUTED BY
15 min active; 2 hr 20 min total	**Four 6-ounce burgers**	**April Bloomfield**

6 oz. ground fatty brisket (see Note)

6 oz. ground short rib

6 oz. ground bottom round

6 oz. ground chuck

Kosher salt

8 oz. Roquefort cheese, crumbled

4 hamburger buns, split and toasted

STEP 1 In a bowl, combine the ground meats, mixing gently with your hands. Divide the meat into 4 pieces and gently shape each into a ¾-inch-thick patty. Set the burgers on a baking sheet, cover with plastic wrap and refrigerate until firm, at least 2 hours.

STEP 2 Light a grill or heat a grill pan. Generously season the burgers on both sides with salt. Grill over high heat until browned outside and medium-rare within, about 3 minutes per side. Transfer to a rack and top each with

2 ounces of the crumbled Roquefort. Let the burgers rest for 3 minutes, then set them on the toasted buns and serve.

Note
Ground skirt steak can replace the ground brisket, the ground short rib or both.

Beef Brasato with Pappardelle & Mint

San Francisco chef Chris Cosentino loves to cook beef shank and oxtail in red wine for a *brasato* ("braised" in Italian) that he serves with mint pappardelle made from scratch. This delicious streamlined version calls for just beef shank, and fresh pappardelle from the store replaces homemade.

TIME **45 min active; 4 hr total, plus overnight marinating**	MAKES **8 servings**	CONTRIBUTED BY **Chris Cosentino**

2¾ lbs. trimmed boneless beef shank, cut into 2-inch pieces

One 750-ml bottle dry red wine

15 mint sprigs, stems reserved

Kosher salt and pepper

¼ cup extra-virgin olive oil

One 35-oz. can peeled Italian tomatoes, crushed

1 lb. fresh pappardelle

4 large garlic cloves, thinly sliced

Freshly grated Parmigiano-Reggiano cheese, for serving

STEP 1 In a large resealable plastic bag, combine the beef, wine, mint stems and a generous pinch each of salt and pepper. Seal the bag and refrigerate overnight.

STEP 2 Preheat the oven to 325°. Drain the beef, reserving the marinade; discard the mint stems. Pat the beef dry. In a large enameled cast-iron casserole, heat 2 tablespoons of the olive oil. Add half of the meat and cook over moderately high heat, turning occasionally, until well browned all over, 12 minutes. Transfer to a plate. Brown the remaining meat over moderate heat.

STEP 3 Return all of the meat to the casserole. Add the marinade and bring to a boil. Add the tomatoes, season with salt and pepper and bring to a boil. Cover and braise in the oven for about 2 hours and 15 minutes, until the meat is very tender.

STEP 4 Using a slotted spoon, transfer the meat to a plate and shred with 2 forks. Boil the braising liquid until reduced to 2½ cups, about 20 minutes.

STEP 5 Meanwhile, in a large pot of salted boiling water, cook the pappardelle until al dente. Drain and return the pasta to the pot. Add the meat and the reduced braising liquid and cook over moderate heat, stirring, until the pasta is well coated with the *brasato*, about 2 minutes.

STEP 6 In a small skillet, heat the remaining 2 tablespoons of olive oil until shimmering. Add the garlic and cook until lightly golden, about 1 minute. Add the mint leaves and cook for 10 seconds. Pour the garlic-mint oil over the pasta and toss. Serve in shallow bowls, passing the cheese alongside.

Griddled Gaucho Steak with Bread & Basil Salad

To turn beef tenderloin into a quick-cooking cut, Argentinean grill guru Francis Mallmann butterflies it first to form a quarter-inch-thick slab. Then, after rubbing the meat with oil and topping it with chives, he sears it for just five minutes in a hot skillet. "I love charring things very, very fast so that they're still raw in the middle," he says. If you aren't comfortable butterflying the tenderloin yourself, ask your butcher to do it.

TIME	MAKES	CONTRIBUTED BY
30 min active; 1 hr total	**4 servings**	**Francis Mallmann**

1 head of garlic

½ cup plus 2 Tbsp. extra-virgin olive oil, plus more for drizzling

2 Tbsp. red wine vinegar

Sea salt and pepper

½ lb. rustic bread, cut or torn into 1½-inch pieces

1 lb. center-cut filet mignon

1 large bunch of chives (1 oz.)

¼ cup basil leaves

1 cup microgreens

STEP 1 Preheat the oven to 425°. Cut ½ inch off the top of the garlic head and set the head on a piece of foil. Drizzle the garlic with olive oil, wrap tightly and roast until tender, about 45 minutes. Unwrap the garlic and let cool slightly, then squeeze the cloves into a small bowl. Mash with a fork until smooth. Whisk in ¼ cup of the olive oil and the vinegar and season the dressing with sea salt and pepper.

STEP 2 Meanwhile, in a large nonstick skillet, heat ¼ cup of the olive oil. Add the bread and cook over moderate heat, tossing, until golden and crisp all over, about 5 minutes. Arrange the croutons on plates.

STEP 3 Using a sharp knife, make a ¼-inch-deep cut down the length of the filet mignon. Turning the filet and rolling it out as you go, spiral-cut the meat until you have a long, rectangular piece that's about ¼ inch thick;

alternatively, have your butcher butterfly the steak for you. Make ½-inch-deep slits every 2 inches along the grain all over the steak. Rub the steak with 1 tablespoon of the olive oil. Season with sea salt and pepper and arrange the chives on top, tucking them into the slits.

STEP 4 Heat a cast-iron skillet. Add the remaining 1 tablespoon of olive oil and cook the steak, chive side up, over moderate heat until browned, about 3 minutes. Flip the steak and cook until the chives are charred and the steak is medium-rare inside, 2 to 3 minutes longer. Transfer the steak to a cutting board and let rest for 5 minutes.

STEP 5 Top the croutons with the basil leaves and microgreens and spoon the roasted garlic dressing on the greens. Slice the steak against the grain and serve alongside.

Bone-In Rib Eye Steaks with Grilled Onion Jam

The combination of sweet and tangy onion jam and garlicky, buttery meat is irresistible. Dan Kluger of Loring Place in New York City says the trick to grilling perfect steak is starting the meat at room temperature and turning it often so it cooks evenly.

TIME **1 hr total**	MAKES **4 servings**	CONTRIBUTED BY **Dan Kluger**

ONION JAM

3 red onions, sliced

Extra-virgin olive oil, for brushing

Kosher salt and pepper

1 cup apple cider vinegar

¼ cup pure maple syrup

¼ tsp. finely chopped thyme

STEAKS

Two 1½-lb. bone-in rib eye steaks (1½ inches thick), at room temperature

Extra-virgin olive oil, for brushing

Kosher salt and pepper

2 Tbsp. unsalted butter, softened

2 tsp. minced rosemary

2 tsp. minced thyme

2 garlic cloves, grated

STEP 1 MAKE THE ONION JAM Light a grill or heat a grill pan. Brush the onions with olive oil and season with salt and pepper. Grill over moderate heat, turning once, until lightly charred and tender, about 7 minutes.

STEP 2 In a medium saucepan, bring the vinegar and maple syrup to a boil. Add the onions and simmer over moderately low heat until tender, about 8 minutes. Transfer to a bowl; let cool. Stir in the thyme. Season with salt and pepper.

STEP 3 MAKE THE STEAKS Light a grill or heat a grill pan. Brush the steaks with oil and season with salt and pepper. Stand the steaks on their fatty edges (bone side up) and cook over moderate heat until the fat has started to render and is lightly charred, about 5 minutes. Lay the steaks flat. Grill, turning often, until an instant-read thermometer inserted in the thickest part registers 120°, 12 to 15 minutes. If using a grill pan,

carefully blot excess fat with paper towels to prevent flare-ups. Transfer to a cutting board; let rest for 10 minutes. Leave the grill on.

STEP 4 In a bowl, blend the butter, rosemary, thyme and garlic. Brush the herb butter on the steaks and grill over high heat, turning once, until sizzling, 1 minute per side. Transfer to a carving board. Slice the steaks and serve with the onion jam.

Mixed Grill with Fresh Tomato & Pepper Salsa

To accompany his wood-roasted beef short ribs, leg of lamb and chorizo, Uruguayan chef Marcelo Betancourt serves a simple salsa called *criolla,* which he makes by marinating tomatoes, onions and bell peppers overnight in lemon juice and olive oil. In addition to the meats here, the salsa is fantastic with any grilled fish or poultry.

TIME	MAKES	CONTRIBUTED BY
1 hr, plus overnight marinating	**6 servings**	**Marcelo Betancourt**

1 medium red onion, cut into ⅓-inch dice

1 medium tomato—halved, seeded and cut into ⅓-inch dice

½ red bell pepper, cut into ⅓-inch dice

½ green bell pepper, cut into ⅓-inch dice

½ yellow bell pepper, cut into ⅓-inch dice

¾ cup extra-virgin olive oil

3 Tbsp. fresh lemon juice

Kosher salt and pepper

2 Tbsp. finely chopped flat-leaf parsley

1½ lbs. boneless leg of lamb roast

1½ lbs. flanken-cut beef short ribs (cut across the bones), about ½ inch thick

1½ lbs. fresh chorizo or hot Italian sausage

STEP 1 In a large bowl, combine the onion with the tomato, bell peppers, olive oil and lemon juice. Add a large pinch each of salt and pepper and mix well. Cover and refrigerate overnight. Stir in the parsley and bring to room temperature before serving.

STEP 2 Light a grill. Season the lamb and short ribs with salt and pepper and let stand for 10 minutes. Grill all of the meats over moderate heat, turning occasionally, until the short ribs are browned and cooked through, about 12 minutes; the chorizo is cooked through, about 15 minutes; and an instant-read thermometer inserted in the thickest part of the lamb registers 130° for medium-rare, 25 to 35 minutes, depending on thickness. Transfer the meats to a platter to rest for 5 minutes.

STEP 3 Season the salsa with salt and pepper. Carve the meats and serve the salsa alongside.

WINE TIP If you can't find Uruguayan Tannat, which would be apropos here, look for a spicy Malbec from Argentina instead.

Tri-Tip Steak with Grilled Scallion, Ginger & Cilantro Relish

Tri-tip is a lean, bang-for-your-buck cut that benefits from a big boost of flavor. The accompanying bold relish, made with smoky charred scallions, fresh chiles and just-grated ginger, gives the steak exactly the oomph it needs .

TIME **35 min active; 50 min total**	MAKES **4 servings**	CONTRIBUTED BY **Kay Chun**

One 1½-lb. tri-tip steak

18 large scallions, 2 thinly sliced

2 Tbsp. canola oil, plus more for brushing

Kosher salt and pepper

1 cup chopped cilantro

2 red Thai chiles, minced

2 Tbsp. fresh lime juice

2 Tbsp. finely grated peeled fresh ginger, plus more for garnish

STEP 1 Light a grill. On a baking sheet, rub the steak and 16 whole scallions with the 2 tablespoons of oil; season with salt and pepper.

STEP 2 Oil the grill grate. Grill the steak over moderate heat for 20 to 25 minutes, turning occasionally, until an instant-read thermometer inserted in the center registers 125° for medium-rare. Transfer the steak to a cutting board and let rest for 15 minutes.

STEP 3 Meanwhile, grill the whole scallions over moderate heat, turning, until lightly charred and tender, about 3 minutes. Transfer 8 of the scallions to a platter. Chop the rest and transfer

to a bowl; let cool. Add the sliced raw scallions, the cilantro, chiles, lime juice and 2 tablespoons of ginger to the bowl; mix well.

STEP 4 Thinly slice the steak across the grain and arrange on the platter. Spoon the scallion relish on the steak and garnish with freshly grated ginger.

Merguez-Spiced Colorado Lamb

Chef Jennifer Jasinski of Rioja in Denver loves to showcase Colorado lamb, which tends to be more richly marbled than imported varieties. She rubs the chops with a fragrant, robust spice blend reminiscent of merguez sausage and serves them with a garlic-and-sherry pan sauce.

TIME **45 min total**	MAKES **6 servings**	CONTRIBUTED BY **Jennifer Jasinski**

1 tsp. sweet smoked Spanish paprika

1 tsp. ground cumin

1 tsp. ground fennel

½ tsp. ground coriander

½ tsp. cinnamon

½ tsp. ground allspice

¼ tsp. cayenne

Six 5-oz. lamb loin chops

¼ cup extra-virgin olive oil

Kosher salt and pepper

4 garlic cloves, minced

2 Tbsp. sherry

Chopped parsley, for garnish

STEP 1 In a small bowl, combine all of the spices. Set aside 2 teaspoons of the spice mixture for the pan sauce. Rub the lamb chops with the remaining spice mixture. Let stand at room temperature for 15 minutes.

STEP 2 In a large cast-iron skillet, heat 2 tablespoons of the oil. Season the lamb with salt and cook over moderate heat until golden and an instant-read thermometer inserted in the center registers 125°, 3 to 4 minutes per side. Transfer to plates; let rest for 5 minutes.

STEP 3 Meanwhile, pour off all but 1 tablespoon of oil from the skillet. Add the garlic and cook over low heat, stirring, for 1 minute. Add the reserved 2 teaspoons of spice mixture and cook, stirring, for 1 minute. Add the sherry and whisk in the remaining 2 tablespoons of oil. Season the sauce with salt and pepper and spoon over the lamb. Garnish with parsley and serve.

WINE TIP

The Mediterranean flavors of lamb and spicy merguez call out for a substantial red from Spain's coast–try a Monastrell from Jumilla, for instance.

Leg of Lamb Shawarma

This grilled lamb is one of Dubai chef Silvena Rowe's signature dishes. Traditional shawarma is roasted on a spit all day. Her cheater's version starts with butterflied leg of lamb, which cooks for just 20 minutes on each side. Set the meat out whole on a buffet, or slice and serve it in grilled flatbread with dilled yogurt and cucumbers.

TIME **30 min active; 3 hr total, plus overnight marinating**	MAKES **6 to 8 servings**	CONTRIBUTED BY **Silvena Rowe**

1 head of garlic, top fourth cut off

2 Tbsp. extra-virgin olive oil, plus more for drizzling

Finely grated zest and juice of 2 lemons

1 tsp. sweet paprika

1 tsp. ground cumin

1 tsp. ground coriander

½ tsp. cinnamon

Kosher salt and pepper

One 5-lb. butterflied leg of lamb

Grilled flatbread, plain yogurt mixed with dill and sliced cucumbers, for serving

STEP 1 Preheat the oven to 350°. Put the garlic on a double piece of foil and drizzle with olive oil. Wrap the garlic in the foil and bake for about 1 hour and 15 minutes, until very soft.

STEP 2 Squeeze the garlic cloves into a bowl and mash with a fork. Stir in the lemon zest, lemon juice, paprika, cumin, coriander, cinnamon and the 2 tablespoons of olive oil. Add 1 teaspoon of salt and ½ teaspoon of black pepper.

STEP 3 Lay the lamb on a work surface and make ½-inch-deep slits all over the meat. Transfer the lamb to a rimmed baking sheet and spread the spice paste all over, rubbing it into the meat. Cover and refrigerate overnight.

STEP 4 Light a grill. Bring the lamb to room temperature and season with salt and pepper. Grill the lamb fat side down over moderately high heat until charred, about 20 minutes. Turn the lamb and grill for about 20 minutes longer, until an instant-read thermometer inserted in the thickest part registers 130° for medium meat. Transfer the lamb to a work surface to rest for about 15 minutes.

STEP 5 Carve the lamb into thin slices and serve it in grilled flatbread along with dilled yogurt and sliced cucumbers.

Sweet & Spicy Grilled Beef Short Ribs

Flanken-cut short ribs (cut across the bones) are perfect for quick-cooking on the grill until juicy and delectably charred.

TIME	MAKES	CONTRIBUTED BY
45 min total	**4 servings**	**Justin Chapple**

¼ cup packed light brown sugar

1½ Tbsp. kosher salt

1 Tbsp. paprika

1 Tbsp. chili powder

1 tsp. garlic salt

1 tsp. dried oregano

1 tsp. black pepper

3¾ lbs. flanken-style beef short ribs, sliced ⅓ inch thick

Canola oil, for the grate

Lemon wedges and coleslaw, for serving

STEP 1 In a medium bowl, mix all of the ingredients except the short ribs, oil, lemon and slaw. Rub the mixture all over the short ribs and let stand for 20 minutes.

STEP 2 Light a grill and oil the grate. Grill the ribs over high heat, turning once, until nicely charred and nearly cooked through, about 6 minutes. Transfer to a platter and serve with lemons and slaw.

Rosemary–Garlic Lamb Chops

L.A. chef Nancy Silverton adores the garlicky, herb-flecked grilled lamb chops *scottadito* ("burnt fingers"). Here, she adds an extra kick by garnishing the lamb with smoky pimentón de la Vera and little mint leaves.

TIME	MAKES	CONTRIBUTED BY
25 min active; 2 hr 25 min total	**4 servings**	**Nancy Silverton**

½ cup rosemary leaves

8 garlic cloves

Kosher salt and pepper

½ cup extra-virgin olive oil, plus more for drizzling

12 baby lamb chops (about 3 oz. each)

¼ cup small mint leaves and a large pinch of pimentón de la Vera, for garnish

STEP 1 In a blender, pulse the rosemary and garlic cloves with a pinch each of salt and pepper until coarsely chopped. With the machine on, gradually add the ½ cup of olive oil until the rosemary and garlic are finely chopped. Scrape the mixture into a large baking dish and add the lamb chops. Turn the chops so they are well coated. Refrigerate for at least 2 hours or overnight.

STEP 2 Light a grill or heat a grill pan. Season the lamb chops with salt and pepper. Grill over high heat, turning once, until nicely charred outside and medium-rare within, about 6 minutes. Transfer the lamb to a platter and let rest for 5 minutes. Garnish with the mint leaves and pimentón, drizzle with olive oil and serve immediately.

Grilled Lamb Ribs with Cumin & Coriander

Lamb ribs, which are very similar to pork spareribs, are the most inexpensive and unsung part of the lamb, says butcher Tom Mylan, co-founder of The Meat Hook in Brooklyn. Here he combines the sweet and tangy flavors of American barbecue with Middle Eastern seasonings for richly flavored, succulent ribs.

TIME	MAKES	CONTRIBUTED BY
1 hr 30 min active; 3 hr total	**4 to 6 servings**	**Tom Mylan**

¼ cup kosher salt

2 Tbsp. light brown sugar

1 Tbsp. ground cumin

1 Tbsp. ground coriander

1 tsp. freshly ground pepper

½ tsp. cinnamon

Two 2½- to 3-lb. racks of lamb ribs

1 cup apple cider vinegar

2 Tbsp. pomegranate molasses

STEP 1 In a small bowl, mix the salt with the sugar, cumin, coriander, pepper and cinnamon. Transfer 2 tablespoons of the rub to a medium bowl. In a large, shallow baking dish, sprinkle the remaining rub over the lamb ribs, massaging it into the meat. Let stand at room temperature for 1 hour.

STEP 2 Light a gas grill. Whisk the apple cider vinegar and pomegranate molasses into the reserved 2 tablespoons of rub.

STEP 3 Transfer the lamb ribs meaty side down to the grill and cook over moderately low heat, turning once, until lightly charred all over, 7 to 10 minutes. Reduce the heat to low and grill, turning and basting with the sauce every 10 minutes, until the meat is very tender and nicely charred, 1 hour and 30 minutes. Transfer the ribs to a carving board, tent with foil and let rest for 10 minutes. Cut the ribs between the bones and serve.

WINE TIP Syrah fans should also look to the wines of the northern Rhône Valley in France. Hermitage, Crozes-Hermitage and Côte-Rôtie are all made from this spicy grape.

CABERNET SAUVIGNON
& OTHER BIG REDS

CABERNET SAUVIGNON This noblest of noble reds is always the adult in the room, no matter what wine region it's from. Native to France's Bordeaux, Cabernet produces powerful wines with great structure, a tannic backbone that gives them the ability to age for decades. Even the flavors and aromas that the wines exude—cassis, currant leaf, black tea, cigar box—have a certain dignified, occasionally stern air.

In Bordeaux, Cabernet Sauvignon reaches its heights in the Médoc, on the Left Bank (i.e., the western side) of the Gironde estuary. The soil here is gravelly, and from it the wines derive their focused austerity. While bottles from top châteaus can be extraordinarily expensive (albeit excellent), bottles from satellite areas like the Haut-Médoc or the Côtes de Bordeaux can offer terrific value.

Cabernet Sauvignon, of course, is grown widely beyond Bordeaux, too. Italian producers have been working with the grape since the 1970s, using it to give structure to so-called Super-Tuscan wines. California's Napa Valley has been a source for world-class Cabernet since the 1940s, when groundbreaking winemakers like Inglenook's John Daniel, Jr., produced bottlings that are still incredible today (if you can find them). Under the California sun, Cabernet develops riper fruit characteristics than it does in Bordeaux, but it still has the tannins that enable the wines to age. The same is true of Cabernets from Australia's Coonawarra and Barossa regions, and Colchagua in Chile. Washington state's Columbia Valley has also achieved a reputation as a premier source for stellar Cabernet.

Pairing Cabernet with a dry-aged T-bone (or really any superb steak) is classic for good reason: The wine's tannins give it an unparalleled gift for slicing through the fattiness of well-marbled red meat. But Cabernet doesn't have to be saved for high-end choices. A good Cabernet is an excellent partner for pork ribs, hamburgers or sausages off the grill, too.

MERLOT This variety is Cabernet Sauvignon's more easygoing pal, its sidekick. The two coexist in Bordeaux, with Cabernet prevalent on the region's Left Bank and Merlot reaching dominance on the Right Bank, in the prestigious subregions of St-Émilion and Pomerol. (There's actually more Merlot than Cabernet planted throughout Bordeaux by a fair percentage.) While Merlot also has substantial tannins, they're softer than those in Cabernet, meaning the wines feel smoother earlier on. In fact, Merlot is often blended into Cabernet-based wines to give a rounder mouthfeel overall. Merlot is known for black cherry and plum flavors, and can often have a cocoa powder or even mocha aspect, depending on where it's grown. While not nearly as widely planted as Cabernet (there's more Cabernet in the world than any other red grape), Merlot is often planted in the same regions. Thanks both to Cabernet's fame and the rising popularity of Pinot Noir, these days Merlot tends to be underappreciated, but a great bottle of Merlot can be a perfect partner for a wide range of richer foods, particularly braised meats or pasta with meat sauce.

ZINFANDEL A grape with many names, Zinfandel originated in Croatia, but given its Croatian name—Crljenak Kaštelanski—it's no surprise that Italian and Californian growers decided to call it something a touch more pronounceable. In southern Italy's Apulia it's known as Primitivo and in the US it's Zinfandel, but no matter where this peppery variety is grown, it tends to have an ebullient fruitiness that recalls raspberries and blackberries, always edged with a little brambly spice. Bold and often jammy, Zinfandels are unbeatable when it comes to barbecued chicken and meat—almost anything, in fact, that comes off the grill.

Pork Tenderloin with Sage, Garlic & Honey

Mimi Thorisson, creator of the blog Manger, lives in a 19th-century villa surrounded by some of the greatest vineyards in the Médoc wine region in Bordeaux. This herbaceous pork tenderloin, finished with a touch of honey and butter, is one of her go-to dishes to pair with the area's extraordinary reds.

WINE TIP The wines of Bordeaux's Left Bank, where Thorisson lives, are typically Cabernet Sauvignon–based; they are ideal with roasts like this one.

TIME **35 min active; 1 hr 30 min total**	MAKES **4 servings**	CONTRIBUTED BY **Mimi Thorisson**

½ tsp. freshly grated nutmeg

One 1½-lb. pork tenderloin, cut in half crosswise and tied (have your butcher do this)

Kosher salt and pepper

3 large garlic cloves, thinly sliced

12 sage leaves

3 Tbsp. unsalted butter

3 Tbsp. extra-virgin olive oil

½ medium onion, thinly sliced

1 small carrot, sliced

2 thyme sprigs

1 bay leaf

½ cup dry white wine

1 cup chicken stock

2 Tbsp. honey

STEP 1 Rub the nutmeg all over the pork and season generously with salt and pepper. Tuck the garlic and sage under the strings and let the pork stand at room temperature for 30 minutes.

STEP 2 In a large, deep skillet, melt 2 tablespoons of the butter in the oil. Add the pork and cook over high heat, turning occasionally, until browned all over, about 7 minutes. Transfer to a plate.

STEP 3 Pour off all but 2 tablespoons of fat from the skillet. Add the onion, carrot, thyme, bay leaf and a generous pinch each of salt and pepper. Cook over moderately high heat, stirring occasionally, until the vegetables are softened and browned, 3 to 5 minutes. Add the wine and simmer for 1 minute. Add the stock and bring to a boil. Return the pork to the skillet, cover and braise over low heat, turning occasionally, until an instant-read thermometer inserted in the pork

registers 135°, 13 to 15 minutes. Transfer the pork to a carving board; let rest for 10 minutes.

STEP 4 Meanwhile, strain the braising liquid; discard the solids. Return the liquid to the skillet and bring to a simmer. Remove from the heat; whisk in the honey and remaining 1 tablespoon of butter. Season the sauce with salt and pepper.

STEP 5 Discard the string from the tenderloin, slice the meat and serve with the sauce.

Baked Macaroni with Mortadella & Mozzarella

Paul Kahan of The Publican in Chicago turns up the dial on baked pasta with this maximalist version. He packs it with fresh mozzarella, mortadella, boiled eggs and a rich pork ragù. The grated Parmigiano on top gives it an irresistible, can't-stop-eating-it crust.

TIME **45 min active; 2 hr total**	MAKES **4 to 6 servings**	CONTRIBUTED BY **Paul Kahan**

¼ cup extra-virgin olive oil

1 onion, finely chopped

1 garlic clove, minced

1 lb. ground pork

1 cup dry white wine

One 28-oz. can crushed tomatoes

Generous pinch of crushed red pepper

Kosher salt

2 large eggs

¾ lb. elbow macaroni

2 Tbsp. finely chopped basil

2 Tbsp. finely chopped parsley

One ¼-lb. piece of mortadella, cut into small dice

1 lb. fresh mozzarella, cut into bite-size pieces

1 cup freshly grated Parmigiano-Reggiano cheese

STEP 1 In a large saucepan, heat the oil until shimmering. Add the onion and garlic and cook over moderately high heat, stirring, until softened, 4 minutes. Add the ground pork and cook, breaking up the meat, until browned, about 10 minutes. Stir in the wine and cook until evaporated, 3 minutes. Add the tomatoes, crushed red pepper and a generous pinch of salt and bring to a boil. Cook over moderately low heat, stirring, until thickened, 1 hour.

STEP 2 Meanwhile, in a small saucepan, cover the eggs with water and bring to a boil. Cook over moderately high heat for 8 minutes. Drain the eggs and cool under running water, then peel and finely chop.

STEP 3 Preheat the oven to 425°. In a large saucepan of salted boiling water, cook the macaroni until al dente; drain well and stir into the sauce along with the basil, parsley, chopped eggs, mortadella, three-fourths of the mozzarella and ¾ cup of the Parmigiano-Reggiano.

STEP 4 Transfer the macaroni to a 3-quart ceramic baking dish and scatter the remaining mozzarella and Parmigiano-Reggiano on top. Bake for about 25 minutes, until hot. Let the baked macaroni stand for 5 minutes before serving.

Prep Ahead

The unbaked assembled macaroni can be refrigerated overnight. Let return to room temperature before baking.

Pizza Vesuvio

This pizza-calzone hybrid, served at Rustic restaurant in the Francis Ford Coppola Winery in Sonoma County, is a veritable flavor bomb. Half the dough is folded over, with mozzarella, ricotta, ham and salami tucked inside. On the outside is more mozzarella and ham along with artichokes, mushrooms and olives.

TIME	MAKES	CONTRIBUTED BY
30 min active; 1 hr total	**One 12-inch pizza**	**Francis Ford Coppola**

½ cup frozen artichoke hearts, thawed and sliced ½ inch thick

Extra-virgin olive oil, for drizzling

Kosher salt and pepper

All-purpose flour, for dusting

½ lb. pizza dough, thawed if frozen

¼ lb. fresh mozzarella, cut into 1-inch cubes

2 oz. thinly sliced baked ham, cut into 1-inch strips

½ cup fresh ricotta cheese (4 oz.)

2 oz. salami, cut into 1-inch strips

½ tsp. dried oregano

¼ cup plus 2 Tbsp. marinara sauce

2 large cremini mushrooms, sliced ¼ inch thick

4 pitted olives, sliced ¼ inch thick

STEP 1 Set a pizza stone in the oven and preheat the oven to 500°. Let the stone heat for 30 minutes. In a bowl, lightly drizzle the artichoke hearts with olive oil. Season with salt and pepper.

STEP 2 On a floured work surface, roll or stretch the pizza dough to a 12-inch round, about $\frac{1}{8}$ inch thick. Roll the edge on half of the dough $\frac{1}{16}$ inch thick. Generously flour a pizza peel. Transfer the dough to the peel and lightly brush with oil. Top the thinner side of the dough with half of the mozzarella and ham and all of the ricotta and salami, 3 inches from the edge. Sprinkle with half of the oregano and drizzle with 2 tablespoons of the marinara. Lift the 3-inch edge of dough over the filling and press to seal in the center of the round.

STEP 3 Spread the remaining $\frac{1}{4}$ cup of marinara over the dough, leaving a $\frac{1}{2}$-inch border. Arrange the remaining mozzarella and ham over the marinara. Scatter the artichoke hearts, mushrooms and olives on top. Sprinkle with the remaining oregano.

STEP 4 Slide the pizza onto the hot stone and bake for 8 to 10 minutes, until crisp and bubbling. Cut into wedges and serve.

Slow-Cooked Pork Shoulder with Roasted Apples

WINE TIP

Pork shoulder is a fatty cut, which is why it's so tender after long, slow roasting. As a result, it needs a substantial, tannic red like Cabernet.

This cut of pork roasts in the oven for hours, but the prep is minimal and the results are outstanding: super-crispy skin and meltingly tender meat. Oregon Master Sommelier Nate Ready, who makes his own wine under the Hiyu label, likes to pair it with a robust Napa Cabernet.

TIME	MAKES	CONTRIBUTED BY
45 min active; 8 hr 15 min total	**6 to 8 servings**	**Nate Ready**

One 9-lb. skin-on, bone-in pork shoulder

8 bay leaves

1 Tbsp. juniper berries

Kosher salt and pepper

6 baking apples, such as Gala, quartered and cored

¼ cup extra-virgin olive oil

3 small cinnamon sticks

STEP 1 Preheat the oven to 400°. Using a sharp knife, score the pork skin in a crosshatch pattern. Set the pork in a large roasting pan, skin side up.

STEP 2 In a spice grinder, combine the bay leaves with the juniper berries, ¼ cup of salt and 2 teaspoons of pepper and grind into a powder. Rub the spice mixture all over the pork and into the scored skin. Roast the pork until lightly browned, 30 minutes. Reduce the oven temperature to 325° and roast for about 6½ hours longer, until the pork is very tender and the skin is crisp. Transfer to a carving board and let rest for 30 minutes.

STEP 3 Meanwhile, on a large rimmed baking sheet, toss the quartered apples with the olive oil and cinnamon sticks and season generously with salt and pepper. Roast the apples for about 30 minutes, tossing once, until they are lightly browned and softened slightly. Discard the cinnamon sticks.

STEP 4 Remove the pork skin and coarsely chop it. Using 2 forks, pull the pork into large pieces, discarding the fat and bones. Transfer the pork to a platter and scatter the chopped skin on top. Serve with the roasted apples.

Pan-Roasted Veal Chops with Cabernet Sauce

WINE TIP Use an affordable (but drinkable) bottle for the recipe–then break out a Cabernet you've been saving to serve with the dish.

"If you are a bona fide chef, you have to understand wines. And that is especially true for the *saucier*," says chef Robert Wiedmaier of Marcel's in Washington, DC. Here, he demonstrates his wine knowledge with a luscious Cabernet reduction. To make it even more complex, replace the beef stock and flour with demiglace (concentrated veal stock).

TIME **20 min active; 1 hr 20 min total, plus overnight marinating**	MAKES **4 servings**	CONTRIBUTED BY **Robert Wiedmaier**

¼ cup plus 2 Tbsp. extra-virgin olive oil

4 thyme sprigs

1 garlic clove, coarsely chopped

Four 12-oz. bone-in veal rib chops

2 cups Cabernet Sauvignon

2 large shallots, finely chopped

1 Tbsp. unsalted butter

2 Tbsp. all-purpose flour

2 cups beef stock

Kosher salt and pepper

STEP 1 In a large, shallow dish, combine ¼ cup of the olive oil with the thyme sprigs and garlic. Add the veal chops and turn to coat with the marinade. Refrigerate overnight.

STEP 2 In a medium saucepan, combine the wine with half of the chopped shallots and boil until the wine has reduced to ½ cup, about 15 minutes.

STEP 3 In a small saucepan, melt the butter. Add the remaining shallot and cook over moderately high heat, stirring, until golden, about 3 minutes. Stir in the flour. Slowly whisk in the stock until smooth, then bring to a boil, whisking until thickened. Whisk in the reduced wine and simmer over low heat, whisking, for 30 minutes. Strain the sauce into the medium saucepan. Season with salt and pepper.

STEP 4 Preheat the oven to 325°. In a large skillet, heat the remaining 2 tablespoons of olive oil until shimmering. Remove the veal chops from the marinade; discard the thyme and scrape off the garlic. Season the chops with salt and pepper and add to the skillet. Cook over high heat until richly browned, about 3 minutes per side. Transfer the skillet to the oven and roast the chops for about 10 minutes, turning once halfway through; the veal should be just pink in the center. Transfer the chops to plates, spoon the sauce on top and serve.

Note
If you're using demiglace, you can buy it online from dartagnan.com.

Prep Ahead
The wine sauce can be refrigerated for up to 3 days. Reheat gently.

Pepper-Crusted Skirt Steak with Charred Leeks

Freshly cracked spices give Food Network star Alex Guarnaschelli's skirt steak a wonderful complexity; mustard and vinegar add a delicious tang. The easiest way to crack whole peppercorns and coriander seeds is to crush them under a flat-bottomed skillet. Put the heel of your hand in the skillet, then push down and out away from you.

TIME	MAKES	CONTRIBUTED BY
45 min active; 3 hr 45 min total	**4 to 6 servings**	**Alex Guarnaschelli**

4 Tbsp. unsalted butter

2 tsp. coarsely cracked coriander seeds

2 tsp. coarsely cracked black peppercorns

2 tsp. coarsely cracked white peppercorns

¾ tsp. crushed red pepper

1 Tbsp. packed dark brown sugar

Kosher salt

2 lbs. skirt steak, cut into 5-inch lengths

4 medium leeks (2½ lbs.), white and light green parts only, halved lengthwise and cleaned

2 Tbsp. Dijon mustard

2 Tbsp. balsamic vinegar

3 Tbsp. canola oil

2 Tbsp. fresh lemon juice

STEP 1 In a small skillet, melt the butter. Add the coriander, all the peppercorns and the crushed red pepper and cook over moderately low heat for 1 minute. Scrape into a medium bowl and stir in the brown sugar and 1½ tablespoons of salt. Rub the mixture all over the steak and transfer to a baking dish. Cover with plastic wrap and refrigerate for 3 hours.

STEP 2 In a large saucepan of salted boiling water, blanch the leeks until just tender, 3 to 4 minutes. Using tongs, transfer them cut side down to a paper towel–lined baking sheet to drain.

STEP 3 In a small bowl, whisk the mustard with the vinegar.

STEP 4 In a large cast-iron skillet, heat 1 tablespoon of the canola oil over high heat until smoking. Add half of the steak and cook over high heat, turning a few times, until lightly charred on the outside and medium-rare within, 4 to 5 minutes total. Transfer to a carving board, spread with some of the Dijon vinegar and let rest for 10 minutes. Repeat with 1 tablespoon of the oil and the remaining steak and Dijon vinegar.

STEP 5 Wipe out the cast-iron skillet and heat the remaining 1 tablespoon of oil in it. Add the leeks cut side down and cook over high heat until lightly charred on the bottom, about 3 minutes. Transfer to a platter and drizzle with the lemon juice. Slice the steak against the grain and serve with the leeks.

Swedish Meatballs

"When I was little, I thought these meatballs were huge, but now I think they only seemed that way to a small child," says Magnus Nilsson of Fäviken in Järpen, Sweden. His grandmother's secrets to the ultra-tender texture? Milk-and-cream-soaked breadcrumbs and a cooked potato.

TIME **50 min total**	MAKES **18 meatballs**	CONTRIBUTED BY **Magnus Nilsson**

1 medium baking potato (8 oz.), peeled and cut into 2-inch pieces

1 large egg, beaten

⅓ cup plus 1 Tbsp. whole milk

⅓ cup plus 1 Tbsp. heavy cream

¾ cup plus 2 Tbsp. plain dry breadcrumbs

12 oz. ground beef

12 oz. ground pork

1 small onion, finely chopped

2 tsp. kosher salt

½ tsp. ground white pepper

4 Tbsp. unsalted butter

Mashed potatoes and lingonberry jam, for serving

STEP 1 In a small saucepan, cook the potato in salted boiling water until tender, about 12 minutes. Drain well, then pass through a ricer into a bowl. Let cool.

STEP 2 Meanwhile, preheat the oven to 425°. In a large bowl, whisk the egg with the milk and cream. Stir in the breadcrumbs and let stand for 5 minutes to soften. Add the beef, pork, onion, salt, pepper and riced potato and mix just until combined. Shape the mixture into 18 meatballs.

STEP 3 In a large ovenproof nonstick skillet, melt 2 tablespoons of the butter. Add half of the meatballs and cook over moderate heat, turning, until golden all over, about 8 minutes. Transfer to a plate and wipe out the skillet. Repeat with the remaining 2 tablespoons of butter and meatballs.

STEP 4 Return all of the meatballs to the skillet, transfer to the oven and bake until cooked through, about 10 minutes. Arrange the meatballs on a platter and serve with mashed potatoes and lingonberry jam.

Make Ahead
The uncooked meatballs can be refrigerated overnight.

Chorizo Poached in Red Wine

To make this easy and crowd-pleasing party snack, simply simmer smoky dry Spanish chorizo with garlic in red wine until it's plump and juicy.

TIME **15 min active; 40 min total**	MAKES **10 servings**	CONTRIBUTED BY **Jim German & Claire Johnston**

Two 4-oz. pieces of dry Spanish chorizo

6 cups dry red wine (about two 750-ml bottles)

10 garlic cloves, peeled

4 bay leaves

¼ tsp. cayenne

STEP 1 In a large skillet, combine all of the ingredients and bring to a boil. Cover and simmer over moderately low heat, turning the chorizo once, until plump, about 15 minutes. Uncover and let stand for 5 minutes.

STEP 2 Transfer the chorizo to a work surface and slice on the diagonal ¼ inch thick. Return the chorizo slices to the skillet and simmer over low heat for 5 minutes. Transfer the chorizo slices to a shallow serving bowl and pour in enough of the poaching liquid to reach halfway up the side. Serve the chorizo with toothpicks.

Grilled Strip Steaks with Onion Wedges

This steak is ideal for entertaining because it can be cooked ahead of time. Right before serving, put the medium-rare meat back on the grill just until the surface is hot.

TIME **35 min total**	MAKES **4 servings**	CONTRIBUTED BY **Tim Love**

Two 12- to 14-oz. New York strip steaks, about 1¼ inches thick, at room temperature for 30 minutes

1 white onion, cut into 8 wedges through the core

Canola oil, for brushing

Kosher salt and pepper

STEP 1 Light a grill or heat a grill pan. Brush the steaks and onion wedges with oil and season with salt and pepper. Using tongs, rub 1 of the onion wedges all over the grate or grill pan. Add the steaks and remaining onion wedges to the grill, cover and cook over moderately high heat, turning once, until the steaks are just medium-rare and the onion is tender, 6 to 7 minutes total. Transfer the steaks and onion to a cutting board and let rest for at least 10 minutes.

STEP 2 Return the steaks to the grill and cook, turning once, until the surfaces are just hot, about 2 minutes total. Transfer the strip steaks to the cutting board, slice them across the grain and serve with the grilled onions.

Beef Sirloin with Piquillo Peppers & Capers

Meat expert and cookbook author Bruce Aidells creates a fantastic, bare-bones steak rub with nothing more than paprika, brown sugar, salt and pepper. Jarred roasted piquillo peppers give his genius sauce a smoky sweetness.

TIME	MAKES	CONTRIBUTED BY
30 min total	**4 servings**	**Bruce Aidells**

2 tsp. sweet paprika

1 tsp. dark brown sugar

Kosher salt and pepper

1½ lbs. sirloin steak (about 1¼ inches thick)

¼ cup olive oil

3 garlic cloves, thinly sliced

2 medium shallots, thinly sliced

1 Tbsp. drained capers

1 tsp. chopped fresh sage

8 piquillo peppers (Spanish roasted peppers), seeded and chopped

1 tsp. Dijon mustard

½ tsp. Worcestershire sauce

STEP 1 In a small bowl, mix the paprika, brown sugar, 2 teaspoons of salt and 1 teaspoon of pepper. Pat the mixture all over the meat.

STEP 2 In a small skillet, heat the olive oil over moderate heat. Add the garlic, shallots and capers and cook until softened, about 3 minutes. Stir in the sage and cook for 1 minute. Add the piquillos, mustard and Worcestershire; simmer over moderate heat for 15 minutes, stirring occasionally.

STEP 3 Meanwhile, light a grill or heat a grill pan. Grill the steak over moderately high heat for about 12 minutes, turning once, until an instant-read thermometer inserted in the thickest part registers 130° for medium-rare meat. Let the steak rest for 5 minutes, then slice and serve with the piquillo-pepper sauce.

Beef Tenderloin with Tomatoes, Shallots & Maytag Blue

Cookbook author Marcia Kiesel roasts tomatoes and shallots to intensify their flavor. They're an excellent accompaniment to a lean cut of meat such as beef tenderloin. She dots blue cheese crumbles on top of the finished dish for an extra hit of umami.

TIME	MAKES	CONTRIBUTED BY
40 min active; 1 hr 30 min total	**4 servings**	**Marcia Kiesel**

2 pints cherry tomatoes, halved

1½ lbs. medium shallots, peeled

1 cup dry red wine

3½ Tbsp. extra-virgin olive oil

4 thyme sprigs

Kosher salt and pepper

One 2-lb. center-cut beef tenderloin

2 Tbsp. vegetable oil

4 oz. Maytag blue cheese, crumbled into ½-inch chunks (1 cup)

STEP 1 Preheat the oven to 350°. Spread the tomatoes and shallots on separate rimmed baking sheets. Add ½ cup of the wine, 2 tablespoons of the olive oil and 2 thyme sprigs to the tomatoes. Add the remaining 1½ tablespoons of olive oil and 2 thyme sprigs to the shallots. Season the tomatoes and shallots with salt and pepper, toss well and spread in even layers. Bake for about 40 minutes, until the tomatoes and shallots are very tender. Discard the thyme.

STEP 2 Increase the oven temperature to 425°. Season the tenderloin with salt and pepper. In a large ovenproof skillet, heat the vegetable oil until shimmering. Add the tenderloin and cook over high heat until browned, about 4 minutes. Turn the tenderloin and cook for 3 minutes. Transfer the skillet to the oven and roast for 10 minutes. Turn the tenderloin and roast for 10 minutes longer, until an instant-read thermometer inserted in the thickest part of the

meat registers 125° for medium-rare. Transfer the tenderloin to a carving board and let rest for 10 minutes.

STEP 3 Pour off the fat in the skillet. Add the remaining ½ cup of wine and boil until reduced by half, scraping up the browned bits, about 3 minutes. Remove the skillet from the heat and stir in the tomatoes, shallots and their juices.

STEP 4 Cut the beef into ⅓-inch-thick slices and transfer them to plates; spoon the tomatoes, shallots and sauce on top. Dot with the blue cheese and serve.

Braised Short Ribs with Root Vegetable Mash

This twist on the traditional British Sunday roast swaps in tender, red-wine-braised short ribs and a root vegetable mash for the usual roast beef and potatoes.

TIME	MAKES	CONTRIBUTED BY **Soho**
2 hr active; 4 hr total	**4 servings**	**Farmhouse, Oxfordshire, U.K.**

SHORT RIBS

2 lbs. trimmed boneless beef short ribs, cut into 8 equal pieces

Kosher salt and pepper

All-purpose flour, for dusting

2 Tbsp. canola oil

4 Tbsp. unsalted butter

3 slices of bacon, cut into 1-inch pieces

1 head of garlic, halved crosswise

2 onions, quartered

4 shallots, quartered

3 thyme sprigs

2 bay leaves

2 cups dry red wine

¼ cup ruby port

4 cups chicken stock or low-sodium broth

ROOT VEGETABLE MASH

5 Tbsp. unsalted butter

½ lb. carrots, peeled and cut into ½-inch pieces

½ lb. rutabaga, peeled and cut into ½-inch pieces

½ lb. butternut squash, peeled and cut into ½-inch pieces

½ lb. parsnips, peeled and cut into ½-inch pieces

½ lb. celery root, peeled and cut into ½-inch pieces

6 garlic cloves, crushed

3 thyme sprigs

2 bay leaves

3 Tbsp. honey

1 Tbsp. chopped parsley, plus more for garnish

Kosher salt and pepper

STEP 1 MAKE THE SHORT RIBS Season the short ribs with salt and pepper and lightly dust with flour. In a large enameled cast-iron casserole, heat the oil. Add the ribs and cook over moderately high heat, turning, until browned all over, about 8 minutes. Transfer the ribs to a plate. Add the butter, bacon, garlic, onions, shallots, thyme sprigs and bay leaves to the casserole and cook over moderate heat, stirring occasionally, until the bacon fat is partially rendered and the vegetables are golden, 5 minutes. Stir in the red wine and port and cook over moderate heat until reduced by half, about 5 minutes.

STEP 2 Return the short ribs and their juices to the casserole, add the stock and bring to a simmer. Cover and cook over low heat until the meat is very tender, about 2 hours. Transfer the short ribs to a plate. Strain the sauce through a fine sieve set over a bowl,

pressing on the solids; discard the solids. Return the sauce to the casserole and simmer until reduced by one-third, about 15 minutes. Add the ribs and simmer gently until warmed through, 5 minutes.

STEP 3 MEANWHILE, MAKE THE MASH In a large saucepan, melt 4 tablespoons of the butter. Add the vegetables, garlic, thyme and bay leaves and cook over moderately low heat, stirring occasionally, until the vegetables begin to soften, 10 minutes. Stir in the honey, cover and cook until softened, 15 minutes. Add 1 cup of water, cover and cook, stirring occasionally, until almost all of the liquid is absorbed, 20 minutes longer. Discard the bay leaves and thyme sprigs. Stir in the remaining 1 tablespoon of butter and mash with a fork until chunky. Fold in the 1 tablespoon of parsley and season with salt and pepper. Keep warm.

STEP 4 Spoon the mash onto plates and top with the short ribs. Garnish with parsley and pass the remaining sauce at the table.

Beef Stir-Fry with Fresh & Pickled Ginger

WINE TIP

Cheng likes to serve his own Hestan wines with this dish, but any robust Napa Valley red will work well.

Stanley Cheng, owner of Hestan Vineyards, loves to eat this super-flavorful stir-fry with the blackberry-rich Cabernet from his Napa Valley winery: The firm tannins in the wine are a fantastic match for the gingery hoisin and oyster sauces.

TIME	MAKES	CONTRIBUTED BY
20 min active; 35 min total	**4 servings**	**Stanley Cheng**

MARINADE

3 Tbsp. dry sherry

2 Tbsp. soy sauce

2 tsp. cornstarch

1¼ lbs. sirloin steak, thinly sliced

SAUCE AND STIR-FRY

½ cup low-sodium chicken broth

2 Tbsp. dry sherry

3 Tbsp. oyster sauce

1 Tbsp. hoisin sauce

1½ tsp. Chinese chile-garlic sauce

1½ tsp. cornstarch

3 Tbsp. vegetable oil

¼ cup julienned fresh ginger

6 scallions, cut into 2-inch lengths

2 Tbsp. pickled ginger, sliced into thin strips

STEP 1 In a large bowl, whisk the sherry with the soy sauce and cornstarch. Add the steak and turn to coat with the marinade. Let stand for 15 minutes.

STEP 2 In a small bowl, whisk the chicken broth with the sherry, oyster sauce, hoisin sauce, chile-garlic sauce and cornstarch.

STEP 3 Lift the beef from the marinade; discard the marinade. Heat a wok or large skillet until very hot. Add 2 tablespoons of the vegetable oil and heat until shimmering. Add the steak and stir-fry over high heat until browned and cooked to medium, about 1 minute. Transfer the steak to a plate. Add the remaining 1 tablespoon of vegetable oil to the wok. Add the fresh ginger and scallions and stir-fry over high heat until fragrant, about 30 seconds. Return the steak to the wok and add the pickled ginger and the sauce. Stir-fry until the sauce thickens, about 10 seconds. Transfer the steak to bowls.

Serve With
Steamed white rice or cooked lo mein noodles.

Salt-Crusted Rack of Lamb

For perfectly cooked racks of lamb, chef Mourad Lahlou of Aziza in San Francisco packs them in herbed salt. The salt crust insulates the meat, allowing it to roast evenly, yet mysteriously doesn't add a salty flavor. For the best results, Lahlou positions a remote probe thermometer in the meat before roasting to achieve a beautiful, rosy medium-rare.

TIME	MAKES	CONTRIBUTED BY
20 min active; 50 min total	**4 to 6 servings**	**Mourad Lahlou**

6 cups kosher salt

½ cup coarsely chopped tarragon

1¼ cups cold water

3 Tbsp. extra-virgin olive oil, plus more for serving

Two 1½-lb. frenched racks of lamb

Flaky sea salt, such as Maldon, for serving

STEP 1 Preheat the oven to 350°. In a large bowl, stir the kosher salt and tarragon into the water. The mixture should be slushy; if you squeeze a handful, it should just hold together. At either end of a large roasting pan, using half of the salt mixture, form 2 ovals slightly larger than the lamb racks.

STEP 2 In a large skillet, heat the 3 tablespoons of olive oil. Add the lamb, meaty side down, and cook over moderately high heat until browned, about 4 minutes. Turn the racks and brown the tops and sides for 2 minutes each. Set the racks on the beds of salt and let the lamb cool slightly.

STEP 3 Pat the remaining salt mixture over and around the lamb racks to cover the meat completely. Roast for 25 minutes, until an instant-read thermometer inserted in the center of the meat registers 135°. Remove from the oven and let rest for 5 minutes.

STEP 4 Remove the salt crust and brush any remaining salt off the meat. Brush the lamb with olive oil, then cut into single chops for serving. Sprinkle with flaky sea salt.

Serve With
Sautéed Swiss chard.

Irish Lamb & Turnip Stew

April Bloomfield of The Breslin in New York City loves the clean, simple flavors in this hearty stew. She finishes the dish with lots of chopped parsley and mint. While mint isn't traditional in Irish stew, Bloomfield loves the bright freshness it adds to lamb.

TIME	MAKES	CONTRIBUTED BY
45 min active; 3 hr total	**8 servings**	**April Bloomfield**

3 Tbsp. extra-virgin olive oil, plus more for the roux

3½ lbs. boneless lamb shoulder, cut into 2-inch pieces

Kosher salt and pepper

2 small yellow onions, quartered

8 garlic cloves, crushed

6 Tbsp. all-purpose flour

1 cup dry white wine

4 cups chicken stock or low-sodium broth

3 small turnips, peeled and quartered

½ lb. medium carrots, cut into 2-inch pieces

8 fingerling potatoes (¾ lb.)

3 Tbsp. heavy cream

Chopped parsley and mint, for garnish

Crusty bread, for serving

STEP 1 In a large enameled cast-iron casserole, heat the 3 tablespoons of olive oil until shimmering. Season the lamb with salt and pepper. Working in 3 batches, cook the lamb over moderate heat until browned all over, about 8 minutes per batch. Transfer to a large plate. Add the onions to the casserole and cook over moderate heat, stirring, until golden, about 5 minutes. Add the garlic and cook, stirring, until golden, about 2 minutes; transfer to the plate.

STEP 2 Remove the casserole from the heat and add enough oil to make 6 tablespoons of fat. Whisk in the flour, then return the casserole to the heat. Add the white wine and bring to a simmer over moderate heat, scraping the bottom of the casserole. Stir in 4 cups of water along with the chicken stock and whisk until smooth and simmering, then add the lamb and onion mixture and bring to a simmer. Cover and cook over moderately low heat, stirring occasionally, until the lamb is tender, about 1 hour and 45 minutes.

STEP 3 Add the turnips, carrots and potatoes to the casserole and cook over moderately low heat until tender, about 30 minutes. Stir in the heavy cream; season with salt and pepper. Ladle the stew into bowls and garnish with chopped parsley and mint. Serve with crusty bread.

Make Ahead
The stew can be refrigerated for up to 3 days.

Index

Photo Credits

Contributors

HUGH ACHESON is the chef and owner of Five & Ten and The National in Athens, Georgia, and Empire State South and Spiller Park Coffee in Atlanta.

BRUCE AIDELLS is the founder of Aidells Sausage Company and the author of several cookbooks, most recently *The Great Meat Cookbook*.

JOSÉ ANDRÉS is the chef and owner of Jaleo in Washington, DC and several other restaurants in cities worldwide, including Las Vegas, Los Angeles, Miami Beach, Mexico City and Dorado, Puerto Rico.

CATHAL ARMSTRONG is the chef and owner of Restaurant Eve, Eamonn's, PX and Hummingbird, all in Alexandria, Virginia.

BANK ATCHARAWAN is a co-owner of The Patio Desserts & Drinks in Las Vegas.

JIMMY BANNOS, JR., is the chef and co-owner of The Purple Pig in Chicago.

MARIO BATALI is the chef and co-owner of Babbo in New York City and more than a dozen other restaurants in cities worldwide, including Las Vegas, Los Angeles and Newport Beach, California, New Haven and Westport, Connecticut, and Singapore. He is also co-owner of Eataly in Manhattan, Chicago and Boston, with a forthcoming location in Los Angeles.

PAUL BERGLUND is the chef at The Bachelor Farmer in Minneapolis.

MARCELO BETANCOURT is the chef at Vik Retreats in José Ignacio, Uruguay.

JAMIE BISSONNETTE is a co-chef and co-owner of Coppa and Little Donkey in Boston, and Toro in Boston, New York City and Bangkok.

RICHARD BLAIS is the chef and co-owner of Juniper & Ivy in San Diego and a judge on *Top Chef*.

APRIL BLOOMFIELD is the chef and co-owner of The Spotted Pig, The Breslin, The John Dory Oyster Bar, Salvation Taco and White Gold, all in New York City, as well as Tosca Cafe in San Francisco.

DANNY BOWIEN is the chef and co-founder of Mission Chinese Food in San Francisco and New York City.

STUART BRIOZA is the chef and co-owner of State Bird Provisions and The Progress, both in San Francisco.

ANNE BURRELL is the host of Food Network's *Worst Cooks in America*. She is a co-owner of Phil & Anne's Good Time Lounge in Brooklyn.

ATHENA CALDERONE is the creator of the food and lifestyle blog EyeSwoon.

KATIE CALDESI is a co-author of several cookbooks and a co-owner of two restaurants and a cooking school in England.

ANDREW CARMELLINI is the chef and co-owner of The Dutch Miami in Miami Beach; Rec Pier Chop House in Baltimore; and several restaurants in New York City, including The Dutch, Locanda Verde, Lafayette and Leuca.

JUSTIN CHAPPLE is an F&W Test Kitchen senior editor, the talent behind the *Mad Genius Tips* videos on foodandwine.com and the author of *Mad Genius Tips*.

STANLEY CHENG is the CEO of Meyer Corporation and the owner of Hestan Vineyards in Napa Valley.

MICHAEL CHIARELLO is the chef and co-owner of Bottega in Napa Valley and Coqueta in San Francisco.

SANJEEV CHOPRA is the chef of Taj Hotels, Resorts and Palaces in India.

ASHLEY CHRISTENSEN is the chef and owner of Poole's Downtown Diner, Beasley's Chicken + Honey, Chuck's, Fox Liquor Bar, Bridge Club and Death & Taxes, all in Raleigh, North Carolina.

KAY CHUN is a recipe developer based in New York City.

MELISSA CLARK is a staff food writer for the *New York Times* and the author of dozens of cookbooks; her latest is *Dinner: Changing the Game*.

CHAD COLBY was formerly the chef at Chi Spacca in Los Angeles.

JESSE ZIFF COOL is the overseeing chef and owner of Flea St. Café and Cool Café at MBP in Menlo Park, California, and Cool Café at Stanford University.

FRANCIS FORD COPPOLA, the acclaimed film director, screenwriter and producer, is the owner of the Francis Ford Coppola Winery in Geyserville, California.

CHRIS COSENTINO is the chef and co-owner of Cockscomb and Boccalone in San Francisco; Acacia House in St. Helena, California; and Jackrabbit in Portland, Oregon.

DIANE CU is a co-publisher of the blog White on Rice Couple and a co-author of the cookbook *Bountiful*.

NAOMI DUGUID is a food writer and cookbook author based in Toronto. Her latest book is *Taste of Persia*.

TYLER FLORENCE is the owner of Wayfare Tavern in San Francisco and co-owner of El Paseo in Mill Valley, California.

ERIN FRENCH is the chef and owner of The Lost Kitchen in Freedom, Maine.

DYLAN FULTINEER is the chef at Rappahannock and Rapp Session, both in Richmond, Virginia, and Merroir in Topping, Virginia.

INA GARTEN is the author of numerous cookbooks and the host of Food Network's *Barefoot Contessa*.

SHAWN GAWLE is the pastry chef at Quince and Cotogna restaurants in San Francisco.

JIM GERMAN was a co-owner of the now-closed Jimgermanbar in Waitsburg, Washington.

SPIKE GJERDE is the chef and co-owner of Woodberry Kitchen, Artifact Coffee, Parts & Labor, Grand Cru, Canning Shed and Sandlot, all in Baltimore.

SUZANNE GOIN is the chef and co-owner of several restaurants in Los Angeles, including Lucques and A.O.C.

ALEX GUARNASCHELLI is the chef at Butter in New York City.

CARLA HALL is a co-host of ABC's *The Chew* and the owner of Carla Hall's Southern Kitchen in Brooklyn.

MAGGIE HARRISON is the winemaker and co-owner of Antica Terra winery in Dundee, Oregon.

SOPHIE HEAULME is the owner of Casa Olivi in Treia, Italy.

LINTON HOPKINS is the chef and co-owner of Restaurant Eugene, Holeman and Finch Public House, H&F Burger, Hop's Chicken and the forthcoming C. Ellet's, all in Atlanta.

VIVIAN HOWARD is the chef and co-owner of Chef & the Farmer and Boiler Room in Kinston, North Carolina.

DANIEL HUMM is the chef and co-owner of Eleven Madison Park, Made Nice and The NoMad restaurant, all in New York City.

CHRISTOPHER ISRAEL was the chef and owner of the now-closed Grüner in Portland, Oregon.

MELISSA RUBEL JACOBSON is a recipe developer based in Rye, New York.

JENNIFER JASINSKI is the chef and co-owner of Rioja, Bistro Vendôme and Euclid Hall Bar and Kitchen, all in Denver.

AMANDA JOHNSON was formerly the pastry chef and co-owner of Our Town Bakery in Hillsboro, North Dakota.

CLAIRE JOHNSTON was a co-owner of the now-closed Jimgermanbar in Waitsburg, Washington.

JUDY JOO is the chef and owner of Jinjuu in London and Hong Kong. She hosts the Cooking Channel's *Korean Food Made Simple* and is the author of a cookbook of the same name.

PAUL KAHAN is the chef and co-owner of several restaurants in Chicago, including Blackbird, The Publican and Dove's Luncheonette.

MARCIA KIESEL, a former F&W Test Kitchen supervisor, co-authored *The Simple Art of Vietnamese Cooking.*

KRISTEN KISH is a chef based in Boston and the author of *Kristen Kish Cooking.*

DAN KLUGER is the chef and co-owner of Loring Place in New York City.

IAN KNAUER is the founder of The Farm Cooking School in Titusville, New Jersey.

JESSICA KOSLOW is the chef and owner of Sqirl in Los Angeles.

MOURAD LAHLOU is the chef and owner of Aziza and Mourad in San Francisco.

ALEX LARREA is the chef at Experimental Beach Ibiza, a restaurant and bar on the Spanish island of Ibiza.

DAVID LEBOVITZ is a Paris-based pastry chef, cookbook author and creator of an eponymous blog.

COREY LEE is the chef and owner of Benu, Monsieur Benjamin and In Situ, all in San Francisco.

LES ARCADES is a restaurant that serves classic southern French food in Biot, a town outside Nice.

TIM LOVE is the chef and owner of several restaurants in Texas, including Lonesome Dove Western Bistro in Fort Worth and Austin, and Queenie's Steakhouse in Denton.

FRANCIS MALLMANN is the chef and owner of numerous restaurants worldwide, including Patagonia Sur in Buenos Aires; Los Fuegos at the Faena Hotel in Miami; and Francis Mallmann at Château La Coste in Provence, France.

TONY MAWS is the chef and owner of Craigie on Main in Cambridge, Massachusetts, and The Kirkland Tap & Trotter in Somerville, Massachusetts.

SKYE MCALPINE is the Venice-based author of the blog From My Dining Table.

JANET MENDEL is the author of several Spanish cookbooks, including *Cooking from the Heart of Spain.* She also writes the blog My Kitchen in Spain.

KRISTEN MIGLORE is the creative director of Food52. She compiled the recipes in the *Food52 Genius Recipes* cookbook.

FERNANDA MILANEZI is the chef at Jamies Wine Bar in London.

TOM MYLAN is a co-founder of The Meat Hook in Brooklyn.

ZOE NATHAN is the chef and co-owner of Huckleberry Bakery & Café, Milo & Olive and Sweet Rose Creamery, and co-owner of Rustic Canyon, Cassia, Esters Wine Shop & Bar and Tallula's, all in Santa Monica, California.

BRYANT NG is the chef and co-owner of Cassia in Santa Monica, California.

MAGNUS NILSSON is the chef at Fäviken in Järpen, Sweden.

JOSEPH OGRODNEK is a co-chef and co-owner of Battersby in Brooklyn.

MICHAEL PALEY is the chef at Central Standard and Café No Sé at South Congress Hotel and Goodall's Kitchen at Hotel Ella, all in Austin.

GRACE PARISI, a former F&W Test Kitchen senior editor, is the culinary content editor for Marley Spoon, a meal delivery service.

JEN PELKA is the owner of The Riddler Champagne bar in San Francisco and founder of Magnum PR.

CLAUDINE PÉPIN, daughter of Jacques Pépin, is the author of several cookbooks, including *Let's Cook French.*

JACQUES PÉPIN, master chef and F&W contributor, is the dean of special programs at Manhattan's International Culinary Center. His most recent cookbook is *Jacques Pépin Heart & Soul in the Kitchen.*

VIET PHAM is a consulting chef at Beer Bar in Salt Lake City.

TODD PORTER is a co-publisher of the blog White on Rice Couple and a co-author of the cookbook *Bountiful.*

NATE READY is a Master Sommelier and winemaker in Oregon.

ERIC RIPERT is the chef and co-owner of Le Bernardin and Aldo Sohm Wine Bar in New York City and chef-adviser for Blue by Eric Ripert in Grand Cayman.

MISSY ROBBINS is the chef and co-owner of Lilia in Brooklyn.

KENNY ROCHFORD is the director of sales and marketing for Kosta Browne Winery and CIRQ Estate in Sebastopol, California.

MICHAEL ROMANO is a retired partner of Union Square Hospitality Group.

SILVENA ROWE is the chef and owner of five Omnia restaurants in Dubai.

SUVIR SARAN is the chef at Único Taco in Long Island City, New York.

JONATHON SAWYER is the chef and co-owner of The Greenhouse Tavern, Noodlecat and Trentina, all in Cleveland.

JANE SIGAL is the France correspondent for *Food & Wine* and the author of several cookbooks, including *Bistronomy.*

NANCY SILVERTON is the chef and co-owner of numerous restaurants, including Chi Spacca and Mozza2Go in Los Angeles and Osteria Mozza and Pizzeria Mozza in L.A. and Singapore.

GAIL SIMMONS is the F&W special projects director and a judge on *Top Chef.*

SOHO FARMHOUSE is a retreat in Chipping Norton, England.

WALKER STERN is a co-chef and co-owner of Battersby in Brooklyn.

CURTIS STONE is the chef and owner of Maude and Gwen in Los Angeles.

JESSE SUTTON was the chef at the now-closed Social Restaurant + Wine Bar in Charleston.

MIMI THORISSON is the author of *A Kitchen in France* and *French Country Cooking* and the blogger behind Manger.

JERRY TRAUNFELD is the chef and owner of Lionhead and Poppy, both in Seattle.

JONATHAN WAXMAN is the chef and owner of Barbuto and Jams in New York City, Adele's and Bajo Sexto in Nashville, Brezza Cucina in Atlanta and Waxman's in San Francisco.

ROBERT WIEDMAIER is the chef and owner of Marcel's in Washington, DC.

MARTHA WIGGINS is the chef at Sylvain in New Orleans.

TANDY WILSON is the chef and owner of City House in Nashville.

RICARDO ZARATE is the chef and owner of Mamacita and Rosaliné, both in Los Angeles.

More books from
FOOD & WINE

Desserts: More than 140 of Our Most Beloved Recipes

From the thousands of standout dessert recipes published by FOOD & WINE over the last 30+ years, the editors have compiled this collection of their all-time favorites. You'll find tried-and-true recipes for every occasion: the best bake-sale cookies and bars, showstopper cakes, lush puddings, irresistible pies and supremely giftable candies.

Master Recipes

An intrepid cook's guide to dishes you've only ever dreamed about making at home, this must-have manual breaks down the best way to DIY everything from beef jerky to babka. With step-by-step instructions and photos, experts share their foolproof methods for over 180 delicious dishes. Along the way, you'll learn indispensable skills like fermenting pickles, making bread and tempering chocolate.

Mad Genius Tips

Did you know that you can poach a dozen eggs in a muffin tin? Or grate ginger with a fork? Or ripen bananas in the oven? Discover clever shortcuts and unexpected uses for everyday tools in a book that's as helpful as it is entertaining. Justin Chapple, the star of FOOD & WINE's Mad Genius Tips video series, shares more than 90 hacks for 100+ easy, fun and delicious recipes.

TO ORDER, CALL 800-284-4145 OR VISIT **FOODANDWINE.COM/ BOOKS**